Queen's Thinkers

Queen's Thinkers

Essays on the
intellectual heritage of a university

edited by
Alvin Jackson &
David N. Livingstone

The publication of this book
has been made possible through
the generous support of
the R.M. Jones Lecture Fund

First published in 2008 by
Blackstaff Press
4c Heron Wharf, Sydenham Business Park
Belfast BT3 9LE

© Foreword, George Bain, 2008
© Introduction, Alvin Jackson and David N. Livingstone, 2008
© Essays, the contributors, 2008
© Afterword, Peter Gregson, 2008

All rights reserved
The editors and contributors have asserted their rights
under the Copyright, Designs and Patents Act 1988
to be identified as the authors of this work.

Typeset by Carole Lynch, County Sligo, Ireland
Printed in Ireland by ColourBooks Limited

A CIP catalogue record for this book
is available from the British Library

ISBN 978-0-85640-803-8

www.blackstaffpress.com
www.qub.ac.uk

Contents

FOREWORD by Sir George Bain	vii
Introduction ALVIN JACKSON AND DAVID N. LIVINGSTONE	1
P.G. Tait, Queen's College and Ulster-Scots Natural Philosophy CROSBIE SMITH	7
James McCosh and the Scottish Intellectual Tradition DAVID N. LIVINGSTONE	19
John O'Donovan and the Development of Celtic Studies MARY E. DALY	31
William Whitla and His Legacy PETER FROGGATT	45
James Thomson and the Culture of a Victorian Engineer PETER J. BOWLER	57
Helen Waddell and Literary Europe NORMAN VANCE	69
Maurice Powicke: Medieval Historical Scholarship and Queen's MAURICE KEEN	83
John Bell and the Quantum World P.G. BURKE	93
Philip Larkin and Belfast Literary Culture EDNA LONGLEY	105
Eric Ashby's Vice-chancellorship of Queen's, 1950–1959 PETER FROGGATT	115

E. Estyn Evans and the Interpretation of the Irish Landscape HENRY GLASSIE	131
David Robert Bates and the Belfast School of Physics ALEXANDER DALGARNO	141
J.C. Beckett and the Making of Modern Irish Historiography ALVIN JACKSON	149
John Blacking and Ethnomusicology MARTIN STOKES	159
Chronicling a University LESLIE CLARKSON	171
AFTERWORD by Peter Gregson	187
ACKNOWLEDGEMENTS	191
INDEX	193

Foreword

QUEEN'S UNIVERSITY

Queen's University Belfast has been part of the fabric of the island of Ireland for more than one hundred and sixty years. In celebrating the work of a selection of 'Queen's thinkers' with a conference of that title, we are also celebrating a university that was founded by Queen Victoria in 1845 as one of three constituent colleges (the others being at Cork and Galway) of the Queen's University in Ireland. The Belfast college opened in 1849 with 20 professors and an intake of 195 students.[1] It was raised to university rank, with its own charter and statutes, in 1908.

Queen's, Belfast, found itself in excellent company. It was a constituent part of the tenth university in the then United Kingdom: the others being the English quartet of Oxford, Cambridge, Durham and London; the Scottish quartet of Edinburgh, Glasgow, Aberdeen and St Andrew's; and Trinity College Dublin. The Belfast college soon established a solid academic reputation. Indeed, given its relatively small numbers, it punched above its weight, as evidenced by some of its early thinkers, such as P.G. Tait, James McCosh and James Thomson.

The Queen's colleges were established, in the words of the founding Act of 1845, for 'the better advancement of learning among *all the classes* of her majesty's subjects in Ireland' (italics mine). But the aspiration to inclusivity suggested by the words I have italicised was not immediately realised. The founding legislation decreed that the colleges should be secular institutions that did not teach religion. Since the Catholic Church saw religion and education as inextricably intertwined, the Synod of Thurles decreed in 1850 that the colleges should be shunned by the laity 'as dangerous to faith and morals'.[2] Indeed, they were described as 'godless', and by the third decade of its existence, only about 4 per cent of those attending the Belfast college were Catholic.[3] Given the social structure of the United Kingdom in the nineteenth century, most of the students came from middle-class homes. And although the first woman student was admitted in 1881 and full rights for women were granted in 1895, only 25 per cent of students were female by 1934, only three women were appointed to lectureships between 1931 and 1945, and the first female professor was not appointed until 1964.

The intervening years have brought many changes. Today Queen's has about 24,000 full- and part-time students on degree programmes and another 8,000 students in the Institute of Lifelong Learning. It has about 3,500 staff, including about 1,400 academic staff. And, as various league tables demonstrate, it stands in the top twenty of over one hundred UK universities for both teaching and research.

Queen's is now a pluralistic and inclusive institution. The student body is spread over the two main communities, broadly in line with the composition of the 16–19 age cohort in Northern Ireland: about 53 per cent of this cohort are Catholic, as are 52 per cent of Queen's students. The university has become an exemplar of fair employment in Northern Ireland, with the Protestant–Catholic proportion in its workforce being 60–40 per cent, broadly the same as that for Northern Ireland as a whole. It is now one of the most socially inclusive universities in the UK, with almost 40 per cent of its students coming from families with incomes below the level that would require them to pay fees. About 60 per cent of students and just over 50 per cent of staff are female, though only about 35 per cent of academic staff are female. Like the rest of higher education, Queen's also has too few women at senior levels, but its award-winning Gender Initiative is tackling this issue and, in doing so, provides a model for other institutions to follow.

QUEEN'S ETHOS

To give the vital statistics of Queen's is relatively easy, but these provide only the barest details about its growth and academic standing. They convey little of the character of the university, its spirit and ethos. The key to Queen's character lies in two apparent dichotomies which have influenced its development and informed its academic activities: a desire to provide both a liberal and an applied education; and a desire to serve both the local community and the global world of scholarship.

Since its beginnings, Queen's has provided both a liberal and an applied education. This dual function is summarised in the legislation that gave birth to the university. The 1845 Act refers to 'the better advancement of learning', a general phrase broad enough to encompass the notion of learning for its own sake, while the Charter of the same year refers to the provision of 'arts, law, physic, and other *useful* learning' (italics mine).

Although educational philosophers and theorists may see a dichotomy in these words, in practice Queen's has not. From the outset, it has offered an education that is both liberal and useful. For example, the 1849 Statutes stipulated that the Faculty of Arts was to have two divisions, one of literature and the other of science. And two part-time chairs were established to 'extend the knowledge of Jurisprudence and English Law for general purposes and not for strictly professional purposes'.[4]

This approach has continued to the present day, with Queen's offering a wide range of subjects embracing both liberal and applied studies. It offers about three hundred degree courses, based on combinations from almost one hundred subjects, ranging from the professional fields of law, medicine and engineering, to venerable scholarly disciplines in the humanities and sciences, to degrees in distinctly twenty-first century subjects such as music technology, film studies, information management, and product design and development. As Lord Ashby, one of the most influential figures in the university's history succinctly phrased it: 'Ever since the twelfth century it has been the business of universities to train students for the professions, and this business is in no way incompatible with the acquisition of general intellectual health.'[5]

Queen's other core value is service to the communities of which it is a part. It fulfils this role in its local community in a great many ways: for example, by training students for the professions and employment more generally, through its links with business, industry and other educational providers, and by being a patron of the arts. Indeed, based on my own experience of employment in one Canadian and five UK universities, I have never known a university so intimately connected with its local community as Queen's.

But Queen's is also part of a global community of scholars where knowledge is more valued for its own sake than for its relevance to the local community. Although most universities have responsibilities both locally and globally, the competing claims are particularly strong at Queen's. Northern Ireland, together with the rest of the province of Ulster, has a highly distinctive regional identity, and the local community has looked to Queen's, particularly when it was the region's only university, to supply its educated elite and to provide teaching and research that contribute directly to the wealth and welfare of the community.

More importantly, Queen's local community is a divided community. The university has tried to remain a civilising influence above the community division. But balancing the competing claims of Protestants and Catholics, unionists and nationalists, and at the same time balancing these claims with the university's intellectual obligations to the international world of scholarship, has often proved difficult. Despite the tensions between them, Queen's continues to pursue the twin tasks of serving both the region and the scholarly world. This is underlined by its current mission statement, which refers to the university 'enhancing educational, economic, social and cultural development in Northern Ireland and throughout the world'.

QUEEN'S THINKERS

The ethos of Queen's is exemplified by the thinkers discussed in this collection, a representative rather than an exhaustive list of Queen's excellence. Given that most of them are male, middle-class and Protestant, and that all came from Great Britain or the island of Ireland, they do not reflect the pluralism and inclusivity that characterises Queen's today. But most contributed to both the liberal and applied agenda, most to the local community, and all to the global world of scholarship.

There are the scientists: P.G. Tait, the mathematician and physicist who worked with Lord Kelvin; the engineer and inventor

James Thomson, Lord Kelvin's brother; two of the twentieth century's greatest physicists – quantum theorist John Stewart Bell and mathematical physicist Sir David Bates; and Eric Ashby, Lord Ashby of Brandon, a botanist who served Queen's as vice-chancellor and chancellor.

We also have distinguished historians Sir Maurice Powicke and J.C. Beckett, who did much to shed light on our past; geographer E. Estyn Evans and archaeologist John O'Donovan, who helped us to understand our landscape, cultural heritage and folk history; John Blacking, an ethnomusicologist of international renown; James McCosh, the influential philosopher who went on to become President of Princeton; Sir William Whitla, a prominent medical man who made an enormous contribution both to the local community and to Queen's; and literary giants Philip Larkin and Helen Waddell. Their achievements – and those of their colleagues – are the real story of Queen's, and have set the standard for the future.

In short, our thinkers epitomise the spirit of Queen's. And there is no better time than now – as we look back on the sesquicentenary of Queen's College in 1995 and forward to the centenary of Queen's University in 2008 – to reflect on the intellectual heritage of the university and to assess its impact on the international world of scholarship and on society more generally.

PROFESSOR SIR GEORGE BAIN
PRESIDENT AND VICE-CHANCELLOR OF
QUEEN'S UNIVERSITY, 1998–2004

---

[1] See Brian Walker and Alf McCreary, *Degrees of Excellence: The Story of Queen's, Belfast, 1845–1995* (Belfast: Institute of Irish Studies, Queen's University Belfast, 1994), 7, 14.
[2] T.W. Moody and J.C. Beckett, *Queen's, Belfast, 1845–1949: The History of a University*, 2 vols (London: Faber & Faber, 1959), 1:97–8.
[3] Ibid., 194.
[4] Ibid., 70.
[5] *Q: A Literary Magazine* 1 (1950): 4.

INAUGURATION OF THE COMMANDERY OF ARDS OF THE ORDER OF ST JOHN, 1952

Introduction

ALVIN JACKSON
DAVID N. LIVINGSTONE

This volume, and the conference upon which it has been based, arose out of a desire to explore the contribution made by the staff and graduates of Queen's University Belfast to the world of research and scholarship. The antiquity and prestige of the university are well known throughout the United Kingdom and Ireland. The intellectual contribution of many living Queen's men and women is evident through their books and articles, their media profiles and their contribution to industry, commerce and the wider economic and cultural revival of Northern Ireland. The history of Queen's is also well documented, with a succession of important studies beginning with T.W. Moody and J.C. Beckett's magisterial two-volume *Queen's Belfast, 1845–1949*, published by Faber & Faber in 1959. What is less clear, except perhaps to specialist scholars, is the contribution made by generations of Queen's thinkers to the moulding of their respective disciplines. This volume is designed to demonstrate the ways in which these thinkers have helped decisively to shape those subjects which still command the curriculum in higher education, and which resonate beyond the academy in the life of the community. Contemporary Queen's is more vibrant than ever, but its energy and achievement are anchored in the work of those world-class Belfast scholars who have gone before.

Queen's was originally founded in 1845 as an effort to create a non-denominational college anchored in, and catering to, the communities of the north of Ireland (colleges were simultaneously founded in Cork and Galway to serve the needs of Munster and Connacht). This Queen's College Belfast was affiliated in 1849 to the new Queen's University of Ireland and was supplied with a suite of elegant Gothic buildings, designed by Charles Lanyon. In 1882 the Royal University of Ireland superseded the Queen's University of Ireland as the degree-awarding body and supervisory authority for Queen's College (and indeed the letters 'RUI' are still visible in some of the buildings of the main quadrangle). In 1908 higher education in Ireland was restructured through the Irish Universities Act, through which measure both the National University of Ireland and Queen's University Belfast were formally inaugurated. The sesquicentenary of Queen's College Belfast fell, therefore, in 1995, while that of the establishment of the Queen's University of Ireland (the first usage of 'Queen's University' in an Irish context) took place in 1999.

Queen's at the beginning of the new millennium is indeed an exemplar of new research and scholarly prestige: the university's admission to the select Russell Group of first-division colleges confirms this standing (if confirmation be needed). The combination of circumstances and anniversaries perhaps make this an appropriate moment to review the university's intellectual achievement.

The first decade of the twenty-first century has seen a renewal of Belfast, and of Northern Ireland, in the wake of the Good Friday and St Andrew's agreements. This decade has also seen the flourishing of Queen's, the improvement of its standing in the universities' league tables, the consolidation of its research performance, and the development and improvement of its campus.

The centenary of the chartering of the Queen's University of Belfast falls in 2008. This combination of the renaissance of the modern Queen's and the anniversaries of its original foundation and chartering make the investigation, indeed commemoration, of its intellectual achievements particularly timely.

With these thoughts in mind, a conference was held in April 2004 in order to examine and showcase the scholarly heritage of the university. The contributions to that event form the basis for this volume and the organisational ideas governing the conference are also relevant in explaining the structure of the book. Neither the conference nor the book were designed to celebrate the great public figures who have been associated with Queen's: many eminent administrators, media figures and other celebrities, politicians, business leaders and figures of influence have been connected with Queen's, either as graduates or members of staff. This volume, and the preceding conference, are about the intellectual and scholarly heritage of the university, and not its (very distinguished) contribution to the public life of the United Kingdom and Ireland. The approach is biographical rather than thematic since the intention is to address the general public, rather than a specialist readership within each scholarly discipline (though, equally, we hope that this latter group will not be disappointed by what they find here).

In planning both the conference and book it quickly became clear that the range of Queen's thinkers worthy of inclusion was very great indeed, and that some hard decisions would have to be made. We acknowledge that we may not always have got these decisions right. Following the precedent of the *New Oxford Dictionary of National Biography* and the *Irish Dictionary of Biography*, we excluded living Queen's luminaries, even though some (such as Seamus Heaney) are of pre-eminent significance. We were aware that one of the great strengths of Queen's was the breadth of its research achievement, and we were keen to represent this: this meant exploring the achievement of eminent figures across the arts and humanities, social sciences, science, engineering and medicine, rather than confining our investigation to one corner of the university's activities. We became quickly aware, too, that the university's scholarly achievement was sustained over the decades: there was no obviously barren era, even when the political context in Ireland and Northern Ireland was most challenging. We were therefore keen to look at the achievements of the Queen's thinkers over the full length of the college and university's history, rather than any narrower time frame. Our selection of individuals is thus suggestive rather than exhaustive, representative rather than comprehensive. It is intended only to give a flavour of accomplishments across the spectrum of academic work, from the natural sciences and engineering to the humanities, from medicine to social science.

Though this volume was inspired by the belief that Queen's University has a particularly rich and under-explored intellectual history, any uncritical celebration would have been (in a sense) a betrayal of the scholarly heritage and values which we were seeking to illuminate. The contributors to the volume were chosen because of their expert knowledge of particular Queen's thinkers, were recruited from across the globe, and given a completely free hand in constructing their assessments. We believe that, cumulatively, the picture constructed is striking and impressive; but the approaches taken by our contributors are individual and distinctive, and their subjects are often revealed as complex and flawed. Nevertheless their collective contributions bear witness to the critical role that the university as an institution has in the cultivation of the scientific, social and imaginative life of the community.

P.G. Tait, Queen's College and Ulster-Scots Natural Philosophy

CROSBIE SMITH

CROSBIE SMITH is Professor of History of Science and Director of the AHRC Ocean Steamship Research Project at the University of Kent, Canterbury.

By all accounts, Peter Guthrie Tait (1831–1901), born and bred in Dalkeith near Edinburgh, was one of the wild men of Victorian science. Fierce looking, with a huge domed forehead, he was notorious for initiating public controversies in the periodical press, usually over battles for scientific priority fought on behalf of his friends and colleagues against 'foreign' – especially German – claimants. Then and now his critics have portrayed him, with some justification, as arrogant, intolerant, chauvinistic, and even bigoted.

Certainly he was passionate in his attacks on Continental competitors and in his defence of *British* science – usually *North British* science, for he rarely visited England after his undergraduate years. Equally, he was passionate in his defence of Christianity – the Christianity of middle-of-the-road Anglican and Presbyterianism rather than evangelical Protestantism – against perceived threats from those who would seek to use forms of Darwinism to promote non-Christian '-isms': materialism, pantheism, agnosticism or atheism.

Tait's father was secretary to the fifth Duke of Buccleuch. The Buccleuch family, whom the famous political economist Adam Smith had once served as tutor, was one of the wealthiest aristocratic families in Scotland. During his early years Peter was a pupil at Dalkeith Grammar School, but following the death of his father, the family moved to Edinburgh. After a year at Circus Place School, he enrolled at Edinburgh Academy in 1841.

The Academy inherited all the values of the Scottish Enlightenment. Its aim was therefore to mould educated, cultured gentlemen. Classical languages and geometry formed the foundations for this kind of liberal education. Then, in the 1840s, it seemed a world away from the raw, marketplace economy of Edinburgh's rival, Glasgow, a rising centre of industrial power, especially in shipbuilding and marine engineering. But the Academy encouraged its own style of intense gentlemanly competition, characterised by fierce battles for top places in the class of any given year. In their later years, former pupils retained this competitive spirit. Even a gentlemanly culture of 'duelling' persisted. And while duels might no longer be decided by swords or pistols, honour might be settled through protracted battles in print, especially in the medium of the periodical press.

Tait's classmates at the Academy had similarly privileged – aristocratic or upper-middle-class – pedigrees and several went on to become distinguished in a variety of Victorian roles. In Tait's own year was Edward Harland, son of a Yorkshire doctor, who took up an apprenticeship from 1845 with the famous Tyneside engineering firm of Robert Stephenson, worked for the equally celebrated shipbuilders J. & G. Thomson on the Clyde, and founded the later-famous shipbuilding yard in Belfast.

A year ahead of Tait at school, James Clerk Maxwell, who belonged to the Galloway land-owning gentry, would form a life-long friendship with Tait in matters of mathematical and experimental physics – better known at the time as natural philosophy. Their long correspondence often exchanged witty comments in Greek or in mathematical language. Also in Maxwell's class was one John Scott. Scott later joined with his father in reinvigorating the family's shipbuilding firm at Greenock on the Clyde by gaining a reputation for building the highest-quality iron steamers, including the first three ships of Alfred Holt's Blue Funnel Line, which displaced the sailing clippers from the China tea run in the 1860s.

For his one session at Edinburgh University (1847–48) Tait enrolled in the two highest of Philip Kelland's mathematical classes and typically entered himself in the uppermost of three divisions in James David Forbes's natural philosophy class, contrary to the professor's advice that his new pupil should begin in the second division.

The following year Tait entered Peterhouse – or St Peter's College – at Cambridge. He and his fellow undergraduate William John Steele, a recent Glasgow University pupil of Professor James Thomson, were soon identified as likely high-flyers in the race to win top position – known as Senior Wrangler – in the mathematical examination, or Tripos. The Mathematics Tripos, indeed, bore more than a passing resemblance to the horse races at nearby Newmarket, even to the extent of serious betting on favourites. Moreover, Cambridge undergraduates usually employed mathematical coaches akin to trainers. Peterhouse undergraduates had William Hopkins, known by his successful reputation as the 'senior wrangler maker'. After a rigorous training regime, Tait emerged as Senior Wrangler in January 1852, with the favourite, Steele, as Second Wrangler. Tait had become only the second Scotsman to make Senior Wrangler and was also the youngest Senior Wrangler on record.

Elected a fellow of Peterhouse, Tait remained two and a half further years in Cambridge. His attempts to establish himself as a mathematical coach met with limited success but his one pupil, previously written off by the experienced Hopkins, emerged ahead of Hopkins's best pupil. This prompted the ever-modest Tait to remark: 'Oh, that's nothing – I could coach a coal scuttle to be Senior Wrangler.'[1]

In collaboration with Steele during this period he drafted *A Treatise on Dynamics of a Particle*, which belonged to a tradition of mathematical textbooks for prospective Cambridge wranglers.[2] Tait commemorated Steele's early death by publishing the work under their joint names in 1856 and in six further editions up to 1900. In later years, however, Tait recalled without enthusiasm the role of Cambridge coaches as that of those who 'spend their lives in discovering which pages of a text-book ... [an undergraduate] ought to read'.[3]

Appointed professor of mathematics at Queen's College Belfast from September 1854, Tait joined a dynamic group of academics that included the chemist Thomas Andrews, the engineer James Thomson (brother of William), and James McCosh (later President of Princeton). As well as conducting his own classes, Tait supplemented the natural philosophy professor's lectures with a voluntary class for honours students interested in the higher parts of dynamics. His teaching method involved not only a regular course of lectures but also tutorial instruction with set exercises and problems followed by individual guidance. As a result he gained a reputation as a clear and systematic teacher.

Tait worked closely with Andrews and undertook calculations in support of the chemist's experimental work on the physical chemistry of gases. He helped in construction of the apparatus and developed his own practical skills in the art of glass blowing. From Andrews he learnt above all the techniques of precision experimentation. These were techniques pretty much unavailable to Cambridge undergraduates: William Thomson (later Lord Kelvin) acquired his experimental skills not during his student days at Peterhouse in the early 1840s, but in the Paris laboratory of Victor Regnault, who was also researching the properties of gases with a view to improving heat engine efficiency.

During his Belfast years, Tait also devoted himself to a thorough study of the Irish mathematician William Rowan Hamilton's *Lectures on Quaternions*.[4] Enthusiasm for this new algebra of complex numbers in more than two dimensions – a radical departure from Cartesian methods – combined with his conviction of its utility in solving physical problems, inspired Tait to begin work on his own *Elementary Treatise on Quaternions*.[5] While he never abandoned the new mathematics, he consistently failed to persuade his contemporaries – especially Thomson and Maxwell – of its worth in natural philosophy.

Tait had become acquainted at Peterhouse with the brothers William Archer Porter and James Porter, sons of a Belfast Church of Ireland clergyman and former pupils of Glasgow mathematics professor James Thomson (father of William and James). The Porter brothers went on to distinguished academic careers and James Porter would later serve as master of Peterhouse (1876–1901). Tait married one of their sisters, Margaret, in October 1857. Together with the appointment of James Thomson (junior) to the Queen's College chair of engineering that year, these social networks prepared the ground for Tait's long association with William Thomson.

These networks also show just how closely intertwined were the cultural contexts of Scottish universities with those of Belfast educational establishments. Long before the establishment of Queen's College, the College Department of the Royal Belfast Academical Institution had been the professional home of a whole cast of political radicals and religious liberals, including James Thomson (senior) before his move to Glasgow. With strong Belfast connections, Thomson was a favourite candidate for the new post of Queen's College Principal in 1845, but the government – doubtless mindful of the Reverend Henry Cooke's evangelical crusades against the Academical Institution for its supposed heresies – appointed a 'safe' clergyman instead.

Although we know comparatively little of Tait's religious and political alignments during his six years at Queen's, his friendships with Andrews, James Thomson and John Stevelly (natural philosophy professor at Queen's and formerly of the Academical Institution) make it likely that his sympathies were with the cultivated liberal elites – often embodied in the Literary Society – rather than with populist evangelical causes such as the Revival of 1859.

When James David Forbes retired in 1860 from the Edinburgh University chair of natural philosophy, Tait competed successfully against six other candidates, including Maxwell. James Clerk Maxwell – nowadays regarded by science as the greatest of all Victorian physicists – had just become the victim of economic downsizing at Aberdeen, brought about by the merger of the two university colleges and the redundancy of one of the two natural philosophy professors. Then, as now, however, the ability to attract students counted for at least as much as research profile. As an Edinburgh newspaper admitted, '[it is the deficiency of] the power of oral exposition [in] Professor Maxwell principally that made the [Edinburgh University selectors] ... prefer Mr Tait'.[6]

Tait had indeed a powerful presence in the lecture room, as J.M. Barrie described:

> I have seen a man fall back in alarm under Tait's eyes, though there were a dozen benches between them. These eyes could be merry as a boy's, though, as when he turned a tube of water on students who would insist on crowding too near an experiment.[7]

Throughout the 1850s James and William Thomson, James Prescott Joule and Maxwell built a new physics centred on the doctrines of conservation and dissipation of energy. But their informal programme had been sketched and articulated only in papers scattered in the scientific and popular periodicals of the mid-Victorian period. A convert to energy physics in the early 1860s, Tait quickly made the science of energy into a crusade. By the close of 1861, he had joined forces with Thomson to produce the *Treatise on Natural Philosophy*.[8] The goal was to embody North British energy physics in canonical form.

Tait's relationship with Thomson was one of continual competitive engagement. In Thomson's later words: 'We never agreed to differ, always fought it out. But it was almost as great a pleasure to fight with Tait as to agree with him.'⁹ Their styles contrasted markedly. All Tait seemed to require was, as he expressed it, 'a few hours' contemplation of a subject, with a pot of beer, and the lurid glare from my pipe showing in the darkness; then I can sit down and write you off a chapter in double quick time'. Thomson could do no such thing, feeling 'a repugnance' to writing 'which is not common'.¹⁰ But they shared an ironic sense of humour.

Known popularly as 'Thomson and Tait' – or 'T&T' in accordance with the style used by the authors to address each other – the *Treatise on Natural Philosophy* took Newton's *Principia* as the sacred text of the natural philosopher and proclaimed the 'true' Newtonian gospel to be founded on the doctrine of energy conservation. A strong preference for engineering and geometrical – visual – modes of expression characterised the work. In the end, however, only one of the projected four volumes was ever written. Tait's original goal of making it, in his words, intelligible 'even to savages or gorillas'¹¹ disappeared as the project became less accessible to a wider audience than mathematical physicists. Much of the blame lay with Thomson, whose other interests – ocean electric telegraphy in particular – delayed publication of the volume until 1867.

During the 1860s John Tyndall, professor of natural philosophy at the Royal Institution in London, allied himself with Thomas Henry Huxley and other enthusiasts for Charles Darwin's theory of evolution. Born in County Carlow to a relatively poor – and staunch – Protestant family, Tyndall had risen largely by his own efforts to represent himself as Michael Faraday's heir to physical science in London. Appropriating energy conservation, Tyndall placed the doctrine alongside evolution as one of the foundations of the new creed of scientific naturalism – a creed directly challenging Oxbridge Anglican academics who had long presented themselves as guardians of the sciences within a framework of Christianity. In so doing Tyndall also tried to take control from the North Britishers who had founded energy conservation largely on the experimental work of Joule. Tyndall thus attempted to construct an alternative hero in the figure of a little-known German physician Julius Robert Mayer.

Taking up the cause of Joule against Mayer, Tait quickly made himself the principal crusader for a North British science of energy in scientific and popular periodicals. Tait's *Thermodynamics*, the first textbook explicitly on the subject, performed the same crusading role for students.[12] A later book, *Lectures on Some Recent Advances in Physical Science*, reiterated many of the claims made on behalf of his friends during the previous decade.[13]

Tait's efforts to promote the science of energy as a natural philosophy in harmony with Christian belief were fully endorsed by his North British allies. But when Tait published (with colleague Balfour Stewart) an anonymous book entitled *Unseen Universe, or Physical Speculation on a Future State*, Thomson and Maxwell expressed their disquiet.[14] Ostensibly directed against the materialistic determinism of Tyndall's notorious 'Belfast Address' to the British Association for the Advancement of Science in 1874,[15] *Unseen Universe* offered a new but highly controversial 'Christian' cosmology.

A *visible* universe in temporal decay formed part of an *invisible* whole. The dissipation of energy – applicable only to the visible – did not appear to operate as a fundamental law. The unseen and eternal whole then provided a rationale for human immortality. It was a unified vision which suggested, to its critics at least, an ultimately self-renewing, pantheistic universe rather at odds with Thomson and Maxwell's decisive separation of the material (and transitory) from the spiritual (and eternal) worlds. *Unseen Universe*, however, reached its fourth edition within a year and its tenth by 1883.

By 1867 Tait had won financial support for the funding of laboratory facilities at Edinburgh University. Closely modelled on Thomson's well-established physical laboratory at Glasgow, Tait's was open to all comers from the natural philosophy class for a voluntary course of practical physics upon payment of a fee of two guineas for the first session. From 1868 until 1870 William Robertson Smith – later subject to a Free Kirk heresy trial and subsequently distinguished as professor of Arabic in the University of Cambridge – served as Tait's laboratory assistant and provided students with systematic teaching in practical physics.

In the early 1870s, Maxwell was preparing the ground for the establishment of the Cavendish Laboratory in Cambridge, an ancient university more accustomed to mathematical texts than laboratory practice. Recruited by Maxwell, Tait presented his results on thermoelectricity in the 1873 Rede Lecture[16] delivered in the university's most sacred space, the Senate House, which had never before been defiled by experimental science.

Tait's experimental work also included research into golf ball impact. Golf, indeed, combined Tait's love of experiment with his love of dynamics, and in a series of articles published in *Nature* (1890–3) he revealed that under-spin provided the great secret of long driving. For the entertainment of his scientific colleagues, indeed, he was known to have attempted a round of golf after dark, deploying phosphorescent golf balls.

Tait's third son, Frederick, was Scotland's champion golfer in 1896 and 1898. A soldier in the Black Watch, Lieutenant 'Freddie' Tait served in the Boer War from 1899, was wounded at Magersfontein, recovered, but was killed instantly at Koodoosberg early in 1900 leading an assault on the Boers' position. Although Tait continued for another year in the Edinburgh chair, he never recovered from the blow. Little more than three months after his retirement, he was laid to rest in the churchyard to the east of St John's Episcopal Church in Edinburgh on 6 July 1901.

CONCLUSION

In his own time, Peter Guthrie Tait chose to parallel the role of Huxley in relation to Darwin: Tait was Thomson's bulldog, prepared to fight any battle, scientific, religious or political, on behalf of his Glasgow colleague. More than that, however, he formed an integral part of a North British scientific intelligentsia, whose members often circulated around academic posts and institutions in Ulster and in Scotland but whose influential networks of science and engineering extended far beyond those shores. Tait's sojourn at Queen's might have been short; his travels south of the Scottish border after 1860 might have been infrequent; his publications – 'T&T' excepted – might not constitute enduring monuments within scientific communities of later years; but viewing his career in the context of his social networks helps us to understand the extent to which scientific practice in the Victorian period was inseparable from the broader cultural agendas that shaped our political, religious and educational institutions in the northern parts of Great Britain and Ireland.

1. Cited in C.G. Knott, *Life and Scientific Work of Peter Guthrie Tait* (Cambridge: Cambridge University Press, 1911), 11.
2. P.G. Tait and William John Steele, *A Treatise on Dynamics of a Particle* (Cambridge: Cambridge University Press, 1856).
3. Cited in Knott, *Life and Scientific Work*, 11.
4. William Rowan Hamilton, *Lectures on Quaternions* (Dublin: Hodges and Smith, 1853).
5. P.G. Tait, *Elementary Treatise on Quaternions* (Oxford: Clarendon Press, 1867).
6. Cited in Knott, *Life and Scientific Work*, 16–17.
7. Ibid., 17.
8. P.G. Tait and William Thomson, *Treatise on Natural Philosophy* (Oxford: Oxford University Press, 1867).
9. Cited in Knott, *Life and Scientific Work*, 43.
10. Crosbie Smith, *The Science of Energy: A Cultural History of Energy Physics in Victorian Britain* (Chicago: University of Chicago Press, 1998), 195.
11. Ibid., 195.
12. P.G. Tait, *Sketch of Thermodynamics* (Edinburgh: Edmonston & Douglas, 1868).
13. P.G. Tait, *Lectures on Some Recent Advances in Physical Science* (London: Macmillan and Co., 1876).
14. P.G. Tait and Balfour Stewart, *Unseen Universe, or Physical Speculation on a Future State* (London: Macmillan and Co., 1875).
15. John Tyndall, '[Presidential] Address', *Report of the British Association for the Advancement of Science* 44 (1874): lxvii–xcvii.
16. P.G. Tait, 'Thermo-electricity', *Nature* 8 (1873): 86–8, 122–3.

James McCosh and the Scottish Intellectual Tradition

DAVID N. LIVINGSTONE

DAVID N. LIVINGSTONE is Professor of Geography and Intellectual History at Queen's University.

James McCosh (1811–1894) must have been delighted that Robert Blakey seemed to prefer fishing to philosophy. Blakey, a newspaper owner and Presbyterian of radical leanings who had come from the north-east of England to take up the first chair of logic and metaphysics at Belfast's Queen's College in 1849, appears to have devoted considerable time to writing four volumes on angling. At any rate, the philosopher found himself dismissed from his professorship, reportedly for persistent failure to turn up to his classes.[1] McCosh was the beneficiary of Blakey's apparent recklessness, for Blakey's enforced departure from Queen's in 1851 opened the door to McCosh's educational career. Contrary to appearances, Blakey was no intellectual lightweight. He was the author of numerous philosophical works which received the acclaim of the prolific French thinker Victor Cousin (1792–1867) in his account of *La Philosophie Écossaise*.[2]

His successor, James McCosh, had also drunk deeply at the wells of Scottish Common Sense philosophy and vigorously promoted that tradition throughout his long career. If Blakey was as good a fisherman as he was a philosopher, McCosh was definitely a better philosopher than a connoisseur of poetry. During his inaugural lecture in 1852 – delivered to the intervening cheers of a lively audience – McCosh's enthusiasm for Francis Bacon's inductive method inspired a psalmodic outburst:

> Bacon, like Moses, led us forth at last,
> The barren wilderness he passed,
> Did on the very border stand
> Of the blessed promised land,
> And from the mountain's top of his exalted wit
> Saw it himself, and shewed us it.[3]

Epic poetry it was not. But McCosh's use of this piece of doggerel by Abraham Cowley (from his 1663 ballad 'To the Royal Society' from *Verses Written on Several Occasions*) served to underscore his profound confidence in Bacon's method. It was only by the rigorous prosecution of induction that science had made progress; precisely the same was true of a properly constituted mental science whose task it was to uncover the 'laws of the human mind'. As he went on:

> As Moses was succeeded by a Joshua, so Bacon has been followed by persons trained under him, who have taken possession of the territory which he described. The comparison might be carried out still further, and it might be maintained, that as when Joshua died there remained very much land to be possessed, so there remain to this day important fields of inquiry to which the Baconian induction has never been applied in a systematic manner.

Indeed the territory over which the Baconian empire might extend was vast. McCosh believed that it was 'possible to produce a metaphysics founded on scientific principles' and that 'the precise nature of the intuitive principles of the human mind must be discovered by induction'.[4] Philosophically, this became McCosh's lifelong passion.

In part McCosh's coming to Belfast was a consequence of the intellectual stature of his first book, *The Method of the Divine Government*, which had been published in Edinburgh in 1850 while he was still ministering to his Free Church congregation at Brechin, Scotland. There, determined as he was to 'rip the mask off the face of the moderate age' and expose its self-satisfactions, he had thrown his weight behind the 1843 Disruption of the Church of Scotland.[5] As with his intellectual predecessor, Thomas Reid, when it came to choosing between the speculations of the high and mighty and the honest-to-goodness common sense of every Tom, Dick and Harry, McCosh knew what side he was on. As Reid had put it more than half a century earlier in his penetrating analysis of what he called 'the intellectual powers of man':

> On the one side, stand all the vulgar, who are unpractised in philosophical researches, and guided by the uncorrupted instincts of nature. On the other side, stand all the philosophers ancient and modern … In this division, to my great humiliation, I find myself classed with the vulgar.[6]

For Reid, this declaration was intended to mark his impatience with the tortured meanderings of so-called geniuses whose speculations led to sceptical absurdities. At the same time it gave voice to his enthusiasm for the epistemic principles that were taken for granted in the common affairs of everyday life.[7] As for McCosh, that 'vulgarity' – that commitment to the fundamental significance of humanity's common sensibility – shaped his life at every turn. It governed his philosophical outlook, religious preoccupations and curricular convictions alike.

It was this rugged, not to say uncouth, power of analysis that manifested itself in McCosh's 1850 volume, which subjected John Stuart Mill's *System of Logic* (London, 1843) to critical scrutiny. To McCosh, ethics was to do with internal motivation, not with external actions. Any ethical theory that applied measurements to mere results was wrong-headed. Moral integrity was not a matter of calculus. It was mistaken to think a person virtuous simply because they happened to do the right thing. Polite society's preoccupations with decorum and civilised conversation should not be confused with true virtue.

The book went down well. Its defence of the supernatural, its updating of William Paley (the English theologian who authored a major work entitled *Natural Theology*), and its tying together of nature, mind and morality all appealed greatly to the Belfast Presbyterian fraternity, who, in the person of the Reverend William Gibson, made sure that it fell into the hands of the Earl of Clarendon. Clarendon, for his part, was reportedly so taken up with it one Sunday morning that he forgot to go to church. Blameworthy though this may have been in the eyes of Belfast Presbyterians, Clarendon doubtless made up for it by offering McCosh the Queen's chair.

McCosh's sixteen years in Belfast were exceptionally fertile. During these years he published a remarkable sequence of critical books, notably *The Intuitions of the Mind* (London, 1860). In these works he built on the foundations of the Scottish tradition to develop what came to be called 'intuitional realism' – a philosophical perspective that sought to navigate a course through the treacherous waters of materialism on the one side, and an airy idealism on the other. It was a route that snaked its way between French sensationalism and German romanticism and at base constituted an attempt to provide a realist, but anti-materialist, account of human intuitions.

McCosh did not use his Belfast years simply to build up an international philosophical profile, however. He threw himself into the affairs of the region in many different ways, pronouncing on the religious revival that swept through Ulster in 1859, devoting himself to the work of the Colportage Society of Ireland, an organisation dedicated to the distribution of religious literature, and labouring long and hard to promote a national system of intermediate education which would enable children with academic talent to secure social mobility and provide a feeder system for the Queen's Colleges.[8]

In 1868 McCosh left Belfast to assume the presidency of the College of New Jersey (subsequently Princeton University), a position he occupied until 1888, though he retained his chair of philosophy there until his death in 1894. His arrival was, as an 1870 freshman put it, 'an electric shock, instantaneous, paralyzing to the opposition, and stimulating to all who were not paralyzed'. And indeed his achievements *were* remarkable. His ability to secure the services of distinguished scholars did much to replace Princeton's parochial character with a professionalism that left it ideally placed to become one of the world's leading universities. He modernised the curriculum, promoted elective courses, instigated graduate research and found funding for laboratory equipment. He was instrumental in building up the university's collections, and in 1873 the Chancellor Green Library, a natural history museum and the John C. Greene School of Science were all founded. He taught regularly too, delivering courses in the history of philosophy and in psychology, and through them influencing figures like the psychologist James Mark Baldwin and the vertebrate palaeontologist Henry Fairfield Osborne.[9] Nor did his scholarly reputation diminish. During his American years, McCosh emerged as a vigorous exponent of a theistic version of evolution, defending the development theory in a sequence of highly successful works.[10]

McCosh, the eleventh president of Princeton, had taken office in 1868, a century after his fellow Scot John Witherspoon. He passed away on 16 November 1894, precisely one hundred years and a day after Witherspoon's death. It was as if 'the shades of Witherspoon, which had symbolically presided at his induction to the presidency, were still in friendly control'.[11]

* * *

There are three arenas in which McCosh made major contributions to American intellectual life. In each case, I believe his Belfast years were crucial to these later developments. The three spheres in which he played a major role are the debate over the religious implications of Darwinism, the development of American psychology, and the forging of a curriculum at Princeton which transformed the College of New Jersey into a major research university.

We turn first to McCosh's encounter with Darwinian evolution. Shortly after his arrival in Belfast, he joined forces with fellow Scotsman George Dickie, then Queen's professor of natural history, to publish *Typical Forms and Special Ends in Creation* (Edinburgh, 1855). By that stage McCosh had already been engaged in independent investigations into plant morphology and had spoken on the subject at several meetings of the British Association for the Advancement of Science.[12] In some ways the McCosh–Dickie volume can be read as both the high watermark *and* the last gasp of empirical natural theology before the challenge of Darwinism. But this would be to underestimate its significance. The book was largely patterned on the research of the anatomist Richard Owen, who believed that organic structures were organised according to transcendental plans and that corresponding structural forms (homologous relations, as they were called) were to be found among different animal families.[13] This idealist system[14] was immensely suited to the McCosh–Dickie project, providing as it did resistance to the onslaught of the Paris materialists.[15] But it also enabled McCosh to negotiate a much more positive response to Darwin than many others who remained wedded to older forms of teleology. If design resided more in archetypal plans than in the specific adaptations of the sort that animated Darwin's investigations, then the causal operations of natural selection could be allowed freer play.

It was, I believe, this work with Dickie in Belfast that laid the ground work for McCosh's later emergence as perhaps the foremost reconciler of evolution and Protestant theology.[16] Writing just a few years after his arrival in the New World, he declared that 'the law of Natural Selection' was in all likelihood one of the forces that had shaped what he called the 'the Organic Unity and Growth of the World'.[17]

What facilitated this accommodation to Darwinism was the form of natural history McCosh had learned during his time at Queen's, where he came to conceive of design in terms other than that of Paley's perfect adaptationism. And the results were culturally significant, for his interventions served, at least for a time, to defuse the explosive potential of Darwin's theories to shake the foundations on which Western civilization had long stood.

Let me turn secondly to what might be called McCosh's 'moral Newtonianism' and its impact on American psychology. As I have already noted, McCosh's philosophy was grounded in the Scottish tradition which sought to bring the moral and mental spheres within the orbit of empirical scrutiny. Recall that David Hume was described as the 'Newton of the moral sciences' and that Thomas Reid was convinced that Newton's principles were as applicable to the mental realm as to the material one.[18] It was during his Belfast years that McCosh vigorously pursued his mission to interrogate, by inductive means, the worlds of moral intuition and emotional expression. The project was to steer a course between a materialistic associationism and the drift towards radical idealism. But McCosh wanted to go even further than the Scots had hitherto gone in grasping the inner dynamics of the human psyche. As he put it in his monumental work *The Scottish Philosophy* in 1875: 'At a time when the Scottish metaphysicians were discoursing so beautifully of moral virtue, there was a population springing up around their very colleges in Edinburgh and Glasgow, sunk in vice and degradation.' The institutions which sought in *practical* ways to relieve the 'misery of the outcast and degraded', however, 'had proceeded from very different influences'. Any philosophy that hoped to embrace 'the facts they contemplate' – he went on – 'must dive deeper into human nature and probe its actual condition more faithfully than the academic moralists of Scotland ever ventured to do'.[19]

The empirical tenor of this whole undertaking profoundly impressed James Mark Baldwin, one of the canonical figures in the New American Psychology and founder of one of the world's first psychological laboratories. A student of McCosh's, Baldwin's early efforts were rooted in the McCosh agenda to integrate experimental science and intuitional realism. And so in his work, the fundamental ties between moral philosophy and the new psychology clearly manifest themselves. Thus Baldwin's *Social and Ethical Interpretations in Mental Development* (New York, 1897) – arguably his most significant publication – begins with an analysis of the 'Person as Ethical Self'.[20] To be sure, as Robert Richards observes, 'Baldwin owed McCosh a debt as an esteemed teacher who had whetted his metaphysical appetite but who could not satisfy it.'[21] Yet it remains the case that the ways in which McCosh moulded Scottish realism during his Belfast years to bring consciousness within the bounds of scientific inquiry had a significant role to play in the genesis of the new American psychology.

My final observations rotate around McCosh's commitment to the Scottish democratic intellect and the shaping of the Princeton curriculum. In 1885 the Nineteenth Century Club in New York City staged 'a gentlemanly showdown' as part of a national debate over the future of higher education. It was to have been a three-way contest between Charles Eliot from Harvard, Noah Porter of Yale and McCosh from Princeton, though Porter bowed out and left the stage to the other two. Eliot's progressivism was challenged by the more traditional McCosh, who revealed his abhorrence of a curricular system where music, French plays and novels could oust mathematics, logic, ethics, political economy and the sciences.[22] There is no need here to adjudicate on the rights and wrongs of either position. What is worthy of remark, though, is that the reforms which took place at Princeton, easing its transition into the twentieth century, owed much to McCosh's dexterity. Working in an environment of ingrained resistance, he smoothed the way for change partly by presenting himself as a moderate force – an image that at once distanced him from a faddish Harvard and a die-hard Yale.

The rhetorical finesse that McCosh had acquired by the mid-1880s was born of experiences a quarter of a century earlier in Belfast. Shortly after his arrival at Queen's he was plunged into a debate over proposed curricular reforms which would curtail the scope of the mental sciences, subjects dealing with what we would now call philosophy and psychology. It was altogether deplorable, he insisted, to think that metaphysics, political economy and jurisprudence could be ousted to make way for French, Italian and modern history. Such proposals rode roughshod over the tried and tested Scottish tradition in which moral philosophy held pride of place and was considered crucial to politics, economics and social theory alike. And so in a printed letter to the secretary of the university he called attention to the situation in France where the 'exclusive study of the material sciences' had become so pernicious that it had prompted none other than Cousin to head up 'a movement which ... ended in the higher institutions of France giving an important place to the study of the human mind'.[23]

In the end McCosh lost this battle in Belfast. But that made him all the more determined that Princeton would not make the same mistake. Indeed, I believe it was these experiences in Belfast that prompted him during his inaugural speech at Princeton to warn of the dangers of too much specialisation. 'Let the student first be taken, as it were, to an eminence, whence he may behold the whole country ... and then be encouraged to dive down into some special place, seen and selected from the height, that he may linger in it, and explore it minutely and thoroughly.'[24]

The strategy that James McCosh devised to chart both his own and Princeton's way though the troubled challenges of Darwinian evolution had its origins in his work with George Dickie at Queen's in the mid-1850s. The remarkable sequence of philosophical works that he published during his Belfast years, in which he brought the principle of induction to bear on the mental, moral and emotional realms, later contributed to the emergence of American experimental psychology. And the curricular philosophy that he articulated at Princeton was a compound product of Scottish philosophical principle and Ulster educational practice. Given the significance of these influences, I think it is not too fanciful to suggest that the presence of the Queen's college flag and crest in the Princeton Chapel to this day bears emblematic witness to this transatlantic association.

1. See T.W. Moody and J.C. Beckett, *Queen's, Belfast, 1845–1949: The History of a University*, 2 vols (London: Faber & Faber, 1959), 1:164.
2. On Blakey, see Henry Miller, ed., *Memoirs of Robert Blakey: Professor of Logic and Metaphysics, Queen's College, Belfast* (London: Trübner, 1879), and Frederic Boase, *Modern English Biography: Containing Many Thousand Concise Memoirs of Persons Who Have Died Since the Years 1851–1900, With an Index of the Most Interesting Matter* (London: Frank Cass, 1965; original 1892–1921), qv Cousin's significance for English-speaking philosophy is the subject of George Elder Davie, 'Victor Cousin and the Scottish Philosophers', *Edinburgh Review* 74 (1986), reprinted in Davie's *A Passion for Ideas: Essays on the Scottish Enlightenment 2* (Edinburgh: Polygon, 1994), 70–109.
3. James McCosh, 'On the Method in Which Metaphysics Should Be Prosecuted', *Belfast Mercury*, Tuesday 13 January 1852; *Belfast News Letter*, Wednesday 14 January 1852.
4. Ibid.
5. The major biography of McCosh is J. David Hoeveler, Jnr, *James McCosh and the Scottish Intellectual Tradition: From Glasgow to Princeton* (Princeton: Princeton University Press, 1981). The quotation is from p. 96. See also William Milligan Sloane, ed., *The Life of James McCosh: A Record Chiefly Autobiographical* (Edinburgh: T. & T. Clark, 1896).
6. Thomas Reid, *Essays on the Intellectual Powers of Man* (1785; reprint, Cambridge, MA: MIT Press, 1969), 129.
7. See Nicholas Wolterstorff, *Thomas Reid and the Story of Epistemology* (Cambridge: Cambridge University Press, 2001); Heiner F. Klemme, 'Scepticism and Common Sense', in *The Cambridge Companion to the Scottish Enlightenment*, ed. Alexander Broadie (Cambridge: Cambridge University Press, 2003), 117–35.
8. This is discussed in William Donald Patton, 'James McCosh: The Making of a Reputation. A Study of the Life and Work of the Rev. Dr. James McCosh in Ireland, from his Appointment as Professor of Logic and Metaphysics in Queen's College, Belfast, 1851, to his Appointment as President of Princeton College, New Jersey, and Professor of Philosophy, in 1888' (PhD thesis, Queen's University Belfast, 1993).
9. See Ronald Rainger, *An Agenda for Antiquity: Henry Fairfield Osborn and Vertebrate Paleontology at the American Museum of Natural History, 1890–1935* (Tuscaloosa and London: University of Alabama Press, 1991).
10. Such works include *Christianity and Positivism* (London, 1871) – the published version of his 1871 lectures at New York's Union Theological Seminary – and *The Religious Aspects of Evolution* (New York, 1888) – the results of the Bedell lectures for 1887.
11. Carlos Baker, 'James McCosh', in Alexander Leitch, *A Princeton Companion* (Princeton: Princeton University Press, 1978).

[12] See, for example, James McCosh, 'Morphological Analogy Between the Disposition of the Branches of Exogenous Plants and the Venation of their Leaves', in *Report of the 22nd Meeting of the British Association for the Advancement of Science, Held at Belfast* (London, 1852): 66–8; McCosh, 'Some Observations on the Morphology of Pines and Firs', in *Report of the 24th Meeting of the British Association for the Advancement of Science, Held at Liverpool* (London, 1854): 99–100.

[13] On transcendental morphology in general and Owen's work in particular, see Philip F. Rehbock, *The Philosophical Naturalists: Themes in Early Nineteenth-Century British Biology* (Madison: University of Wisconsin Press, 1983); Nicolaas A. Rupke, *Richard Owen, Victorian Naturalist* (New Haven, Conn.: Yale University Press, 1994).

[14] This is the term used by Bowler; see Peter J. Bowler, 'Darwinism and the Argument from Design: Suggestions for a Re-evaluation', *Journal of the History of Biology* 10 (1977): 29–43.

[15] See Adrian Desmond, *The Politics of Evolution: Morphology, Medicine, and Reform in Radical London* (Chicago and London: University of Chicago Press, 1989).

[16] See, for example, James R. Moore, *The Post-Darwinian Controversies: A Study of the Protestant Struggle to Come to Terms with Darwin in Great Britain and America, 1870–1900* (Cambridge: Cambridge University Press, 1979), 245–51; David N. Livingstone, *Darwin's Forgotten Defenders: The Encounter Between Evangelical Theology and Evolutionary Thought* (Edinburgh: Scottish Academic Press, 1987).

[17] James McCosh, *Christianity and Positivism: A Series of Lectures to the Times on Natural Theology and Christian Apologetics* (London: Macmillan, 1871), 90–92.

[18] Alexander Broadie, 'The Human Mind and its Powers', in *The Cambridge Companion*, 60–78.

[19] James McCosh, *The Scottish Philosophy, Biographical, Expository, Critical, From Hutcheson to Hamilton* (New York: Macmillan, 1875), 299.

[20] See the discussion in Graham Richards, '"To Know our Fellow Men to do Them Good": American Psychology's Enduring Moral Project', *History of the Human Sciences* 8 (1995): 1–24.

[21] Robert J. Richards, *Darwin and the Emergence of Evolutionary Theories of Mind and Behavior* (Chicago: University of Chicago Press, 1987), 458.

[22] George M. Marsden, *The Soul of the American University: From Protestant Establishment to Established Nonbelief* (New York: Oxford University Press, 1994), 199.

[23] James McCosh, 'The Mental Sciences and the Queen's University in Ireland; Being a Letter to the Secretary of the Queen's University' (private publication by Mayne, Belfast, 1860), 6. This document can be found in vol. 10 of the Thomas Andrews Papers held at Queen's University Belfast.

[24] Cited in Thomas Jefferson Wertenbaker, *Princeton: 1746–1896* (Princeton, NJ: Princeton University Press, 1946), 293.

John O'Donovan and the Development of Celtic Studies

MARY E. DALY

MARY E. DALY is Professor of History and Principal of the College of Arts and Celtic Studies at University College Dublin.

John O'Donovan (1806–1861), first professor of Celtic languages at Queen's College Belfast, has been described as 'the most gifted Celtic scholar of his age',[1] yet he had little formal education. O'Donovan's career encompassed the final years of a centuries-long tradition, when most scholarship relating to Gaelic Ireland – its history, laws, literature and medical lore – survived only in manuscript form, and was transmitted by copying these manuscripts, as if the printing press had not yet been invented. This scribal tradition survived thanks to the patronage of people from very diverse backgrounds: the descendants of ancient Gaelic chieftains, such as Charles O'Conor, or the Young Irelander William Smith O'Brien, and prosperous tenant farmers who gave bed, board and a very modest livelihood to scribes and scholars in return for transcribing manuscripts and teaching their children.[2] But patronage was increasingly moving to an urban setting, to Dublin and Belfast, and one of the most remarkable of the later patrons was the Belfast-man Robert Shipboy MacAdam whose fortune came from the Soho ironworks.

During O'Donovan's life, we can see a further shift from individual patrons to the patronage of learned societies: the Royal Irish Academy; the Irish Archaeological Society; the Kilkenny Archaeological Society (forerunner to the Royal Society of Antiquaries of Ireland); and the Ulster Archaeological Society – whose main funder was Robert MacAdam. And the state gradually assumed a much greater role, initially through the Ordnance Survey (which may have been largely unintentional), then through the Queen's Colleges, and the Commissioners for Publishing the Ancient Laws of Ireland (established in 1852), commonly described as the Brehon Law Commission.

The other important change, which was associated with greater corporate and state support, was the very belated transition of Gaelic scholarship from manuscript to print. John O'Donovan has left thousands of pages in manuscript, notably the Ordnance Survey letters – but these were working notes, not finished texts. His finished work appeared in print in the *Dublin Penny Journal*, the

Ulster Journal of Archaeology, and in books. Finally, whereas the older scribes appear to have been interested mainly in passing material on, with the occasional note in the margins, O'Donovan and his peers went far beyond this: they translated, edited and annotated material, and they subjected their sources to critical investigation in a manner that is consistent with modern scholarly practice.

The Gaelic scribes of the seventeenth to nineteenth centuries were men of modest family background, men with no capital – except what we might nowadays describe as human capital; they were literate, they had some learning, and they were prepared to move around in search of employment. John O'Donovan, born in south Kilkenny, shared many of these characteristics.[3] He was the son of a tenant farmer who rented a larger than average farm, but it would appear that he had difficulty retaining his land. O'Donovan was educated in hedge schools, and in a classical school in Waterford. While still in his teens he became a schoolmaster, a precarious and poorly paid job, but he soon moved to Dublin, following an older brother who was employed as a clerk. O'Donovan enrolled in a classical school, apparently with the intention of studying for the priesthood, and then at some point he became a tutor and scribe, teaching Irish to Lieutenant Thomas Larcom, a junior officer in the Royal Engineers who had been appointed to head the Irish Ordnance Survey. He transcribed manuscripts for James Hardiman, the Commissioner of Public Works, for the princely sum of six shillings a week plus breakfast, and for Myles O'Reilly of the Heath House, Maryboro', apparently for little more than bed and board. Hardiman, author of the *History of Galway* and later of *Irish Minstrelsy*[4] was one of the leading antiquarians of his time, so O'Donovan received some training from him in addition to a tiny income.

This precarious existence became a little more secure in October 1830 when Thomas Larcom recruited O'Donovan as a member of the topographical department of the Ordnance Survey, the department responsible for place names.[5] He remained with the Ordnance Survey, with a short break in 1833, until 1842, when this unit was dissolved. The work of the Ordnance Survey has become much better known in recent years through Brian Friel's play *Translations* (London: Faber & Faber, 1981). Yet Friel's representation of English soldiers imposing ugly anglicised place names on the Irish countryside, ignoring the language and lore of the peasantry, is not supported by the historical evidence; for an accurate account, see John Andrews' *A Paper Landscape* and the Ordnance Survey letter-books, many of which have been published.[6] The topographical department of the Ordnance Survey studied place names, physical features and archaeological remains, using a variety of sources. They asked local people the names of places and physical features; they listened to how place names were pronounced, often by several witnesses; asked what the names meant; and they repeated these exercises with a variety of respondents – Catholic, Protestant, peasant, gentleman, schoolteacher, clergyman, oldest resident etc. Contrary to Friel's fictional account, this fieldwork was not carried out by English soldiers but by Irishmen with a knowledge of the Irish language, and the oral evidence was supplemented with written records, available locally or in Dublin: estate records, parish registers, manuscript sources such as the Down Survey and the annals, and whatever local histories or topographical studies were available. When O'Donovan made his first field trip to County Down in 1834, the occasion of his first visit to Belfast, he began by contacting two local antiquarian scholars, Dr James McDonnell, chairman of the Ulster Gaelic Society, and Robert MacAdam, and he secured a letter of introduction from Dr Crolly, the Catholic bishop. During his travels he called on the Reverend John Dubourdieu, the elderly rector of Dumballyrony and Drumgoolan, the author of the Royal Dublin Society's Statistical Surveys of counties Antrim and Down some decades earlier, and on Mr Neilson, nephew of the late Reverend Dr William Neilson, author of an Irish grammar, who was reputed to have possession of his late uncle's collection of books and manuscripts. He examined the records of the Downshire estate in Hillsborough to check the oldest record of townland names; he looked at old maps of the Parish of Blaris; and he called on local collectors of antiquities, coins, military weapons, urns etc., and on the oldest people in the district. He travelled with his 'box of books', which he used to check against local information; he was eager to borrow a manuscript account of the 1641 rebellion as a source. The parish schoolmaster in Moira, Robert McVeagh, 'abandoned his scholars to box for a few hours' in order to guide John O'Donovan around the parish, showing him twenty-five different raths. Climbing Slieve Donard helped O'Donovan to clear up the situation of Rath Murbhulg in Dalaradia – which he determined was Murlogh Bay in County Down, near Dundrum. He confirmed his theory that Ballykinler meant *'town of the candlestick* (horrid name!)' by reading Harris's *History of the County of Down* (Dublin 1744), which stated that the tithes of that parish were appropriated to Christ Church in Dublin for wax light.[7]

The intellectual contribution to Celtic studies from O'Donovan's years with the Ordnance Survey can be classified under two headings. On the one hand there are the field letters – now preserved in more than one hundred volumes – where he recorded his findings, plus comments on extraneous matters, such as the survival of spoken Irish, or the personalities of his informants. These have provided much raw material for scholars interested in archaeology, folk traditions and local history, though as yet very little use has been made of them for ethnography or social history. John Andrews remarked that 'as he [O'Donovan] worked his way across the country in quest of Irish-language place-names, he found himself evolving into a kind of one-man local-history department'.[8]

Of more immediate importance, the years with the Ordnance Survey provided O'Donovan with the scholarly training that underpinned his major intellectual work. From 1835, the topography department of the Ordnance Survey was directed by George Petrie; it was based at his house in Great Charles Street (off Mountjoy Square), close to the major Dublin libraries, rather than in the Phoenix Park with the remainder of the Ordnance Survey team. Petrie was a well-known artist and archaeologist; other notable members of the team were Eugene O'Curry, who became the first professor of archaeology and Irish history at Newman's Catholic University and O'Donovan's brother-in-law; the poet James Clarence Mangan; and the artists William Wakeman and George Du Noyer. Copying, borrowing and translating manuscripts formed a regular part of their work, and it was through these activities that O'Donovan apparently mastered Old Irish. Petrie knew very little Irish but he owned several important Gaelic manuscripts, which he lent to O'Donovan; indeed, he relied on O'Donovan and O'Curry to inform him of their content.

Petrie set new standards of critical scholarship in Celtic studies. Despite, or perhaps because of his limited knowledge of Irish, he concentrated on interpretation and analysis, not on translation and editing. His 1830 essay on Irish round towers, which won the Royal Irish Academy's Cunningham Medal, the Academy's major honour, rescued them from being seen as Phoenician temples or places of phallic worship, and established that they were much more prosaic bell towers.[9] Petrie performed a similar scholarly function with regard to Tara, and he was instrumental in transforming the *Transactions of the Royal Irish Academy* into a refereed journal subject to high scholarly standards – a change that did not meet with the approval of all of the Academy's members.

Under Petrie's auspices O'Donovan began to publish his scholarly research, beginning with a series of short pieces in the *Dublin Penny Journal*, which was launched in June 1832. Joep Leerssen has described the *Journal* as 'a cultural and historical magazine for the middle classes', which bore 'an unmistakable Petrie-esque imprint, dedicated as it was to the critical and factualist elucidation of Irish antiquity against all undoubted speculation'.[10] O'Donovan published nineteen short papers, consisting of reprints of original material from the annals and other early Irish sources, with glosses and translation.

O'Donovan's greatest achievement was the translation and scholarly edition of *Annála Ríoghachta Éireann*, more commonly known as the *Annals of the Four Masters*: a history of Ireland from Gaelic sources, covering the period from 2242 BCE, or forty days before the great flood, to 1616, compiled by Franciscan friars in Donegal. They were recording the history of a civilization that they believed was disappearing, following the conquest of Ireland in the early seventeenth century, the departure of the Gaelic chieftains, the substitution of Common Law for Brehon Law, and the triumph of the Protestant reformation. O'Donovan was not the first to produce an edition of the annals; Charles O'Conor of Belnagare made a Latin translation from the original Irish, and Owen Connellan, another scribe/scholar, who was a contemporary of O'Donovan, produced an English translation, which was 'put into readable English by Mangan'.[11] O'Donovan was highly critical of both editions, with justification. He approached the task with a much better knowledge of Old Irish, and the ability to identify places and historical references thanks to his long service with the Ordnance Survey. In 1848 he published a three-volume edition of the volume of the annals that Petrie had given to the Royal Irish Academy, which covered the years 1172–1616.[12] His edition of the entire annals – from 2242 BCE to 1172 held in Trinity College Dublin and the later volume held in the Royal Irish Academy – was published in seven volumes in 1851.[13]

O'Donovan's edition of the *Annals of the Four Masters* is one of the defining cultural statements of the Gaelic revival: the typeface, which was designed by Petrie, exercised a major influence on future generations of publications in Irish. O'Donovan was elected to the Royal Irish Academy in 1847, on foot of the soon-to-be published volumes; in 1848 he was awarded the Cunningham Medal, and he received an honorary LLD from the University of Dublin (Trinity College). In 1856 he became an honorary member of the Royal Prussian Academy (the first Irishman so honoured); the citation mentioned the *Annals* and his *Grammar of the Irish Language* which was much used by German philologists.[14]

But these scholarly distinctions did not feed O'Donovan, his wife and his numerous sons. The winding up of the Ordnance Survey topographical team left him without a regular source of income. He received £100 a year from the Irish Archaeological Society, and other sums for copying and editing manuscripts, but this source of income disappeared during the years of the Great Famine; he may have earned a modest fee for the Irish language classes that he conducted in the Royal Irish Academy, where the class of seven included William Smith O'Brien and Thomas Davis. In 1847 he was called to the bar, but Dublin was full of briefless barristers, and he seriously considered emigrating to America, where many of his family had settled. He informed a friend that the publishers had issued the first part of the *Annals*, 'with the sole view of keeping me from starving during the famine, and they succeeded in keeping me alive (nothing more) for which I feel grateful'.[15]

In such circumstances the prospect of a chair of Celtic languages at a Queen's College was extremely attractive. In June 1848, Richard Hitchcock of Trinity College Dublin wrote to John Windele, the Cork antiquarian, that he had been informed that O'Donovan would have a choice of three professorships, adding 'I am sure you feel happy having him located in Cork'.[16] O'Donovan himself anticipated an appointment in Cork, probably because Sir Robert Kane, the president of the college, had already approached him to lecture in Irish.[17] O'Donovan was interested in a chair, rather as a matter of necessity, 'unless I wish to disappear as well as the potatoes and be carried off by *scuab fanaigh*, I must get something to eat; and I see nothing more congenial to my habits, pursuits, notions etc etc than what this "infidel" set offers' (a reference to the Catholic Church's opposition to the Queen's Colleges). He planned to stay in Dublin, working 'at whatever offers', travelling to Cork about four times a year to deliver lectures on Irish language, history, etc.[18] However, in August 1848 John O'Daly, another member of the Dublin Gaelic scholarly fraternity, informed Windele that 'O Donovan is for Belfast; Connellan [Owen Connellan, the editor of an earlier edition of the Annals] for Cork and a Mr Cornelius Mahony [of] whom no one has heard a word in the halls of Irish literature is appointed to Galway! I was cast aside.'[19] O'Donovan claimed that he was too Catholic for Cork; but perhaps he did not pursue the appointment with sufficient enthusiasm.

Belfast had the disadvantage that the president of the college did not wish a chair of Celtic languages (unlike Kane in Cork),[20] but otherwise it offered many attractions for Celtic studies. Breandán Ó Buachalla's 1968 book *I mBéal Feirste Cois Cuan* records the rich tradition of scholarship and scholarly interest in Irish language, literature and cultural heritage from the 1790s until the 1860s, as does Roger Blaney's more recent study of Presbyterians and the Irish language.[21] William Neilson taught Irish at the Royal Belfast Academical Institution (Inst) during the years 1818–21.[22] According to Breandán Ó Buachalla no town in Ireland was doing as much for the Irish language in the years before the Famine; five books in Irish were published in Belfast between 1830 and 1841; the Ulster Gaelic Society, founded in 1828, had an ambitious programme for teaching Irish and publishing easy primers; and Robert MacAdam had assembled an extensive collection of Irish manuscripts, including material on folklore and folk music that he collected while travelling on business throughout the province and beyond. Yet John O'Donovan was not happy in Belfast, though we might suggest that he never stayed there long enough to discover if it was congenial. He had no students, because the subject did not form part of the BA syllabus, but at this time many of the students at the Queen's Colleges were not degree students. He continued to hope for a job in what he described as 'the sunny south', and some of his comments on the Belfast people smack of cultural and racial stereotyping: such as his reference to 'a cold calculating money-saving people, who think that this world is worth enjoying, but to tell you the candid truth, I do not like them half so much as the poetic southerns'.[23] There are many remarks of this nature scattered throughout his letters, although given that many of the comments were addressed to Windele in Cork at a time when he still hoped to move there, perhaps we should treat them with some scepticism. Dublin remained his home; in 1852 he applied without success for the vice-presidency of Queen's College Galway. He travelled to Belfast every year to deliver a series of lectures. In May 1851 MacAdam reported to Thomas Swanton (a Cork antiquarian scholar) that O'Donovan was lecturing twice a week on 'úghdaras na Gaoidheilge agus air a ngaol a tá aici le teangthaibh eile' – (the scholarly provenance of Irish and its relationship with other languages).[24] But he spent most of his time in Dublin, working with O'Curry (then a professor at Newman's Catholic University) for the Brehon Laws Commission on material that was not published until after both their deaths.

One of the issues that O'Donovan's association with Belfast brings into focus is his attitude towards the Irish language. It would appear that he regarded Irish as a dying language, seeing his task not as that of reviving or preserving it as a mass language, but of recording it, studying it and establishing its scholarly credentials, like Latin and Greek, whereas MacAdam and the Ulster Gaelic Society were keen to transmit spoken Irish to the masses. He rejected approaches by MacAdam, who sought his help with establishing a monthly Irish paper, claiming that he was too busy with his manuscripts. Writing to Windele about the Queen's Chair he explained:

> I do not expect to do much in the way of teaching Irish but if I could establish a taste for Historical and antiquarian investigation it would give me much satisfaction ... the Celtic Professorship is a

difficulty. The stipend is too small and it would be difficult to add to it in either of the provincial capitals. The taste for Irish language and literature will become less and less every year, and therefore I think it of more consequence to work steadily and assiduously to preserve in an intelligible form what historical materials we can have than anything that could be done in the way of teaching the language, which will become obsolete in about fifty years ...[25]

O'Donovan often commented on the disappearance of the language; on a number of occasions he blamed young priests for this, but he appears to have regarded its passing as inevitable.[26] However he did join MacAdam and Windele in urging the Census Commissioners to include a question on the Irish language in the 1851 Census, emphasising how important this was 'at a critical period in our history'.[27] Asked in the same year where to find the best Irish speakers, he replied 'in the poorhouse' or dead.[28] None of his nine sons learned to speak Irish in their home, although both parents were Irish-speakers; one picked up Irish later from the German Celtic scholar Kuno Meyer. Indeed O'Donovan would appear to have adopted a very utilitarian attitude to their education, placing the emphasis on maths and science, the study of medicine and entrance examinations for the Indian civil service – not an entirely surprising decision in the light of his precarious financial circumstances. Four of his sons became active Fenians, which created some headaches for Sir Thomas Larcom, who was by then the Irish under-secretary (the most senior civil servant in Ireland); Larcom gave considerable help to the family after O'Donovan's death. However, it would be unwise to see their Fenianism as a consequence of their father's Celtic studies.

I would like to conclude with some brief comments on O'Donovan's scholarship. His scholarly circle was small, rather introverted, and characterised by much feuding, personalised criticism and personal jealousy – e.g. the refusal to hand over copies of manuscripts; vitriolic criticism of the scholarship of one's peers, including O'Donovan's harsh criticism of his brother-in-law O'Curry's lack of scholarship in Latin and Greek.[29] Several writers have remarked that he did not leave any examples of creative writing in Irish; we can go further and say that he left few examples of creative scholarship; his publications consist of transcriptions, translations and scholarly editions of documents; there is very little by way of interpretation. He saw himself as 'a mere quarryman digging from the bowls of antiquity materials for the future poets and historians of Ireland'.[30] His work was an essential first step in putting Celtic studies on a scholarly footing, but I would suggest, hesitantly, that he cast a long shadow. Scholarship in the Irish language, literature and folklore, though not in archaeology, has continued to be unduly dominated by editing and by critical and close study of the texts. With some exceptions, there remains a reluctance to engage in the broader intellectual analysis which offers a way to transmit an understanding of the material to a wider non-expert audience. But we cannot hold O'Donovan responsible for the failings of his successors; instead we should recognise his contribution to placing Celtic studies on a scholarly footing, and making it possible for later generations to gain a wider understanding of the Irish past.

---

[1] T.W. Moody and J.C. Beckett, *Queen's, Belfast, 1845–1949: The History of a University*, 2 vols (London: Faber & Faber, 1959), 1: 63.

[2] See L.M. Cullen, 'Patrons, Teachers and Literacy in Irish: 1700–1850', in *The Origins of Popular Literacy in Ireland: Language Change and Educational Development 1700–1920*, eds. Mary E. Daly and David Dickson (Dublin: Department of Modern History, Trinity College Dublin, 1990), 15–44; Robert Somerville-Woodward, '"Language without a Mouth": The Development of an Irish Language Consciousness, c. 1820–1878' (PhD thesis, University College Dublin, 1999); Meidhbhín Ní Urdail, *The Scribe in Eighteenth- and Nineteenth-century Ireland. Motivations and Milieu* (Münster: Nodus Publikationen, 2000).

[3] See Patricia Boyne, *John O'Donovan (1806–1861): A Biography* (Kilkenny: Boethius, 1987).

[4] James Hardiman, *The History of the Town and County of the Town of Galway: From the Earliest Period to the Present Time* (Dublin: W. Folds, 1820); James Hardiman, *Irish Minstrelsy, or Bardic Remains of Ireland: With English Poetical Translations. Collected and Edited with Notes and Illustrations* (London: J. Robins, 1831).

[5] For a comprehensive account of the Ordnance Survey, see J. H. Andrews, *A Paper Landscape: The Ordnance Survey in Nineteenth-century Ireland* (Oxford: Clarendon Press, 1975).

6. Brian Friel, John Andrews and Kevin Barry, '*Translations* and *A Paper Landscape*: Between Fiction and History', *The Crane Bag* 7 (1983): 118–24; J.H. Andrews, 'Notes for a Future Edition of Brian Friel's *Translations*', *The Irish Review* 13 (1992–3): 93–106.
7. Michael Herity, ed., *Ordnance Survey Letter Down: Letters Containing Information Relative to the Antiquities of the County of Down Collected During the Progress of the Ordnance Survey in 1834 [John O'Donovan]* (Dublin: Four Masters Press, 2001), 12–13, 56, 65.
8. Andrews, *A Paper Landscape*, 127–8.
9. George Petrie, *The Ecclesiastical Architecture of Ireland Anterior to the Norman Invasion; Comprising an Essay on the Origins and Uses of the Round Towers of Ireland, which Obtained the Gold Medal and Prize of the Royal Irish Academy, vol. 1* (Dublin: Hodges and Smith, 1845). For an account of the 1830 prize essay contest see Joep Leerssen, *Remembrance and Imagination. Patterns in the Historical and Literary Representation of Ireland in the Nineteenth Century* (Cork: Cork University Press, 1996), 112–14.
10. Leerssen, *Remembrance and Imagination*, 114.
11. Boyne, *John O'Donovan*, 83–4; quotation is from O'Donovan to Thomas Davis in Charles Gavan Duffy, *Short Life of Thomas Davis 1840–1846* (London: T. Fisher Unwin, 1895), 160, as cited by Boyne, 84; *Annals of Ireland from the Year DCCXCIII to ... CXC from the Scriptores Hiberniae of the Rev. Dr. C. O'Conor, Translated by the Rev. Richard Butler* (Trim: Henry Griffith, 1843); *The Annals of Ireland Translated from the Original Irish of the Four Masters by Owen Connellan, With Annotations by Philip McDermott and the Translator* (Dublin: B. Geraghty, 1846).
12. *Annála Ríogachta Éireann: Annals of the Kingdom of Ireland, by the Four Masters, to 1616*, 3 vols (Dublin: Hodges and Smith, 1848).
13. *Annála Ríogachta Éireann: Annals of the Kingdom of Ireland, by the Four Masters from the Earliest Period to 1616. Edited from Mss. in the Library of the Royal Irish Academy, and of Trinity college Dublin, with a Translation and Copious Notes by John O'Donovan*, 7 vols (Dublin: Hodges and Smith, 1851).
14. John O'Donovan, *A Grammar of the Irish Language: Published for the Use of Senior Classes of the College of St. Columba* (Dublin: Hodges and Smith, 1845).
15. Boyne, *John O'Donovan*, 59, 84, 109.
16. Royal Irish Academy, Windele MSS 4 B 8/88.
17. Boyne, *John O'Donovan*, 92.
18. Letter to Dr William Reeves, DD, Rector, Ballymoney, County Antrim, 1 December 1848, University College Dublin, Special Collections, cited in Boyne, *John O'Donovan*, 93, 180.
19. Royal Irish Academy, Windele MSS 4 B 9/21, John O' Daly Aug 9 1949.
20. See Moody and Beckett, *Queen's, Belfast*, 1:51.
21. Breandán Ó Buachalla, *I mBéal Feirste Cois Cuan* (Dublin: An Clóchomhar Teoranta, 1968); Roger Blaney, *Presbyterians and the Irish language*

(Belfast: Ulster Historical Foundation and Ultach Trust, 1996).
22. Blaney, *Presbyterians and the Irish Language,* 123.
23. Royal Irish Academy, Windele MSS 4 B 10/87, 8 Newcomen Place, 26 November 1850.
24. Ó Buachalla, *I mBéal Feirste Cois Cuan*, 238.
25. Royal Irish Academy, Windele MSS 4 B 9/74, 5 Victoria Place Belfast, 27 February 1850.
26. Royal Irish Academy, Windele MSS 4 B 9/74, 27 February 1850; also Boyne, *John O'Donovan.*
27. Royal Irish Academy, Windele MSS 4 B 10/116, 31 January 1851.
28. Sean O Luing, *Kuno Meyer, 1858–1918: A Biography* (Dublin: Geography Publications, 1991), 78.
29. See Royal Irish Academy, Windele MSS 4 B 17/84 for comments on O'Curry's lack of scholarship and 4 B 20/165 over refusals to lend manuscripts; also Robert Somerville-Woodward, 'Language without a Mouth' from Ó Buachalla, *I mBéal Feirste Cois Cuan*, 84.
30. Somerville-Woodward, 'Language Without a Mouth', 103, citing NLI MS 132 [173].

William Whitla
and His Legacy

PETER FROGGATT

SIR PETER FROGGATT is a former Vice-chancellor and President of
Queen's University and Past President of the British Medical Association.

INTRODUCTION

Five medical practitioners from Ulster have been president of the British Medical Association.[1] Four were professors at Queen's and the fifth (Sir Ian Fraser, president in 1962–3) could have been had he accepted a strong invitation to apply for the vacant chair of surgery in 1947. Two of them, including William Whitla (1851–1933; BMA president in 1909–10), dealt exclusively with medical education in their presidential addresses. A third, in medically prehistoric 1884, considered research but regarded it as ancillary to clinical practice: as his title puts it, 'The control of pathological research by clinical observation'.[2] The bedside and lecture theatre dominated. The fourth Queen's professor to hold the presidency was myself. I did not reflect on these two burning issues in my presidential address; I had a more pressing theme – the skill and fortitude of Northern Ireland's doctors during the thirty-year Troubles.[3]

This small and biased sample might suggest that Queen's emphasised medical education and practice over *clinical* research. And on the face of it, this interpretation would be correct: this was national par for the period, given that *clinical* academic staff were overwhelmingly part-time until the 1950s and could rarely organise research projects. But what is puzzling is that at Queen's, unlike at many other medical schools, this priority still seems to exist. Higher Education Funding Council Research Assessment Exercises (the dreaded RAEs) and their perforce recent antecedents have consistently placed Queen's medical school in the *bottom third* in the UK, while the Quality Assurance and General Medical Council assessments of teaching and examining have equally consistently placed the school in the *top decile*. Furthermore, the clinical skills on daily display in Northern Ireland are unquestioned. Several specialities are internationally acclaimed: trauma, obviously, given our recent history, cardiology notably; but there are others.

In his 1909 BMA presidential address, delivered in Belfast, Whitla uncannily anticipated today's assessments when he said that '… from the moment of its birth the Medical School of Belfast was characterised by an originality of thought, an earnest and a conscientious recognition of its high mission, and an intense practical trend – qualities which ... still remain [in 1909] as its chief distinguishing feature after about a century of patient and noble service'.[4] This rosy view of a school staffed by medical paragons no doubt owes something to Dr Johnson's dictum that 'in lapidary inscriptions a man is not upon oath', but nonetheless the essentials are true. Such doctors would be likely to score well in assessments of teaching, examining and clinical skills; and today's doctors in Northern Ireland, as I have remarked, do just that. Whitla's accolade 'originality of thought' may lift an eyebrow if it were deduced a posteriori from the unexciting clinical, as distinct from the often vigorous non-clinical, research record; rather, I think, it was probably a characteristically generous judgement by Whitla articulated for the benefit of his national audience – not his first and certainly not his last act of courtesy and fraternal benevolence.

These attributes, and especially the 'intense practical trend', are essentially those of today's medical profession in Northern Ireland. Significantly, they were those of Whitla, himself a fortiori. In so describing his colleagues he was also describing himself. Whitla produced no sea change in either the direction or the content of the medical curriculum, nor in investigatory orientation, nor even in the thrust of clinical training – though he talked eminently good sense on all of them. Essentially, he kept the region's medical ship manned by his medical paragons, on its existing course. However, as the first physician of truly worldwide fame from the province of Ulster, and its brightest luminary, he energised the local medical scene to produce a better trained, more confident, more coherent and cohesive, and a much heartened and proud profession. This, and not some wrench on the tiller, was Whitla's great contribution to medicine in Northern Ireland.

WHITLA THE DOCTOR

Whitla was born in Monaghan town in 1851, one of twelve children of a successful pawnbroker and woollen draper. He became a pharmaceutical chemist but soon entered Queen's College Belfast, qualified in medicine with the Edinburgh 'double qualifications' in

1873,[5] was houseman at the Belfast General Hospital (which later became the Royal Victoria Hospital), entered practice locally and soon thrived, took the MD (the Queen's University in Ireland, 1877) with all available honours and thrived even more. After some minor honorary local hospital appointments he became a physician to the General Hospital in 1882. That same year he published the first of his three textbooks, the ground-breaking *Elements of Pharmacy, Materia Medica and Therapeutics* (London: Henry Renshaw, 1882), which went through fourteen editions in sixty-one years, the first eleven, which sold over fifty thousand copies in several languages, being written entirely by himself. Now internationally known, he was appointed in 1890 to the chair of Materia Medica at Queen's, which he vitalised, and two years later published his second bestseller, *A Dictionary of Treatment or Therapeutic Index including Medical and Surgical Therapeutics* (London: Henry Renshaw, 1892). This went through nine editions in forty-seven years, the first three written without any assisting contributor. It appeared in several languages and had American and Chinese editions. It added to his growing reputation and even more to his growing fortune, was mandatory in smaller doctor-less ships in the Royal Navy and Merchant Marine, and sold many tens of thousands of copies. In 1902 he was knighted with the rare citation of 'author and physician', and in 1908 again demonstrated his prodigious energy, publishing his third though least successful blockbuster, *A Manual of the Practice and Theory of Medicine* (London: Henry Renshaw, 1908). This was in two volumes and totalled 1,900 pages, all written by himself, though with much material from his previous two books. It was never re-published, suffering under the dominance in that market of Sir William Osler's classic *Principles and Practice of Medicine* (New York: D. Appleton and Company, 1892), whose first six editions by that time had sold well over one hundred thousand copies.

President of the BMA, twice president of his beloved Ulster Medical Society (1886–7, 1901–02), pro-chancellor of Queen's and much else besides, Whitla retired in 1919. Deeply religious (more on this subject below), he paid John Murray (of London) to republish (in 1922) Sir Isaac Newton's 1733 exegesis *Observations Upon the Prophecies of Daniel and the Apocalypse of St John*, prefaced by his own *Introductory*

Study on the Nature and Cause of Unbelief of Miracles and Prophecy. It met with a mixed critical reception but a distinct lack of public interest – half of the original print run of 1,007 copies were pulped, though it remained in loss-making print until 1943.[6]

Whitla died in December 1933, four years after a debilitating stroke. His wife had died eighteen months previously. There were no children. He made many munificent gifts to the causes he supported and to the local profession, and willed large benefactions to Queen's University and to Methodist College Belfast.

Whitla's intellectual and professional legacies are less clearly definable than his material ones. The runaway success of his first two textbooks was the basis of his international fame and comfortable fortune. Their radical organisation and up-to-the-minute content exactly met the needs of doctor, pharmacist and student and, at a time of great advances in knowledge, of curriculum content and of professional registration requirements. They remained, updated under new authors and editors, sufficiently robust to survive well into the twentieth century. His first book, which was written primarily for students of medicine, was organised radically into five sections based essentially on his philosophy of the importance of various aspects of prescribing: pharmacy, materia medica, therapeutics, administration of medicines, and pharmacopoeial reactions and tests. He appreciated the enlightening effect of therapeutics on materia medica and the development of pharmacology and he linked them together in an easily accessible format. These organisational qualities and presentational skills were also in evidence in his second book and in his teaching. Though not an experimenter himself, he appreciated the value of research, encouraged it, and lectured on its importance – as Professor Robin Shanks, recent holder of Whitla's eponymous chair, has emphasised in his excellent biographical essay.[7] He was a vivid raconteur, and his oratorical and often oracular delivery befitted his dramatic and literary leanings. He was a long-serving president of the Belfast Shakespeare Society, frequent host to Sir Frank Benson and his players, and depicted himself as Corin, the elderly shepherd, in the great stained-glass window portraying a scene from *As You Like It* which he gave to the Medical Institute, a role-model of shepherding sheep which greatly appealed to his evangelising spirit.[8] Widely travelled to medical and cultural centres, he would return laden with artefacts which he distributed generously, including Pio Fedi's sculpture of Galileo, which he donated to the Ulster Medical Society and which now broods over the Queen's entrance hall.

WHITLA THE MAN

Whitla's credentials as a legator are not exclusively medical. A deeply religious man at a time and in a place where religion mattered, he abandoned his family's Presbyterianism on marrying the ardent evangelical Ada Bourne of Staffordshire, though he stopped short of joining her in the Salvation Army and instead settled for Methodism. He was to dedicate his book on Daniel to William Bramwell Booth, General of the Salvation Army and a frequent houseguest. He was prominent as a lay preacher, was chairman of the local YMCA, and served for twenty-seven years as a governor of Methodist College Belfast, to which he bequeathed £10,000 (at least £0.5 million in today's money). He was an unyielding non-denominationalist in tertiary education.[9] He criticised the Irish Catholic hierarchy for anathematising the non-denominational Queen's Colleges and for pursuing their dream of a Catholic university à la Louvain. He criticised Trinity College Dublin for the lateness of its conversion from Anglican exclusiveness to mere Anglican preference. And he criticised the Presbyterian Church in Ireland for eyeing the possibility of exerting an undue influence on the proposed Queen's University of Belfast, as it was doing on Queen's College Belfast.

Whitla practised what he preached. Moral judgements appear in his medical texts; hard work, high ethics and generosity constituted his credo. As he said in 1901 when proposing a Medical Institute for the Ulster Medical Society (the building was completed in 1902 at some £8,000 cost to Whitla), his chief aim was 'the advancement of those great principles on which true progress, honour and dignity of our noble and self-denying profession depend'.[10] He was temperate though not teetotal; was a moderate (pipe-) smoker, and invested (I won't say 'speculated', still less 'gambled') astutely and successfully in the stock market, notably in oil shares.

He was a generous host, enjoyed formal functions and enlivened garden parties and the like by appearing in the full dress regalia of a Deputy Lieutenant, complete with knee breeches, decorative frock coat and sword, and accompanying his wife, dressed in sombre Salvation Army uniform. As was common for one of his background, he was a fervid opponent of Home Rule for Ireland, a signatory of the 1912 Solemn League and Covenant, a (Unionist) member of the fruitless Irish Convention of 1917–18, and was returned to Westminster in 1918 and 1922 in the Unionist interest as the Member for Queen's, retiring in 1923.

COMMENT

Such was the man and his work. I conclude with an opinion on his professional legacies, a comment on his material ones, and a view on the integrity of Ulster medicine as Whitla had originally noted.

I have said that Whitla both embodied and promoted the desirable characteristics he discerned in the Ulster profession. Ulster medicine was, and for many years after Whitla's time remained, a closed circuit – Ulster men, and later women, studied medicine and then practised it in the local fields and streets and staffed the local hospitals and the medical school, and then taught many of the next generation of Ulster students. It seemed to them a virtuous circle well-nigh impregnable. It hardly even mattered where the student studied, and of course in the pre-Queen's Colleges days they perforce studied elsewhere; but the tangled history of medical education in these islands over the past two hundred and fifty years is not for those of a shy or nervous disposition. I have copious statistics to support this virtuous-circle scenario but three examples will suffice. First, in the hundred years from 1849, when the Queen's Colleges opened, to 1949, near enough the start of the modern medical era, some 95 per cent of medical students at Queen's College Belfast (and from 1909 Queen's University) were from Ulster, overwhelmingly from what became the six counties of Northern Ireland. In the academic year 2003–4, the figure is even higher, at 98 per cent (omitting overseas student quotas), though the reasons for such exclusivity are now rather different. Second, during the same hundred years twenty-one clinical medical professors were appointed at Queen's, of whom twenty were from Ulster; the lone immigrant was from London (St Bartholomew's Hospital), and he only made it in 1947.[11] The third statistic – which really bundles together two statistics – is that the *majority* of Queen's medical graduates practise in Northern Ireland and the *great majority* of those practising in Northern Ireland are themselves from Northern Ireland, and before 1950 were almost exclusively so. The local profession, therefore, is spawned by the local society and as such mirrors its values. Traditionally this society has favoured practical skills and provided the robust, self-reliant and unsophisticated milieu of a rural, even frontier, society, which it carried into the period of intense industrialisation and whose members have little appetite for affecting the philosophies and mores of their metropolitan cousins. It is taken by the practicalities, not the abstractions and adornments, of life and scorns many of what are seen as the effete practices and fashionable values of the cultural oligarchies and the 'big house' societies.

Such a society also values education. Clinical, ethical and teaching standards have accordingly always been high, but clinical research has tended to languish, partly because its modern requirements were not easily obtained in provincial isolation in pre-internet days, partly because it was not an obvious priority of the society I have described, and partly because robust individuality, laudable in a 'frontier' society, often led to small teams of as little as one and academic 'departments' hardly much bigger. Furthermore, a common identity and coherence within cultural and religious groups produced a professional cohesion and also an understanding between doctor and patient not always evident in more amorphous societies. Ulster's doctors were never Oxbridge or Pall Mall gentlemen. Nor were they scions of patrician families relying on high birth and patronage for advancement in their careers. They were, quite simply, from the fields and streets of Ulster; and they still are. There has, of course, been potentially vitiating cultural, even at times biological, inbreeding, and favouritism and nepotism were not unknown. Especially in recent years, however, these have been offset sufficiently by talented imports to ensure hybrid vigour. Ulster doctors know their patients because they know themselves. Likewise, William Whitla knew the strengths of the local profession because he knew his own; and he preached, encouraged, husbanded, supported, taught and, finally, endowed those people and institutions which promoted the qualities he himself possessed, thereby, as he saw it, ensuring their betterment.

WHITLA THE BENEFACTOR

His benefactions tell it all. As well as the Medical Institute for the Ulster Medical Society, built in 1902, he willed (in 1933) his elegant residence and spacious grounds to Queen's to use as the vice-chancellor's residence and made the university his residuary legatee, which amounted to some £35,000 to be used to build 'either an Assembly Hall or a men's hostel'. In the event both were possible and the legacy funded the Whitla Hall and the former forty-two-study/bedroom Queen's Chambers in Queen's Elms, where the Students' Union now stands. Whitla did not directly endow his former chair, as is generally supposed. In 1965 the Medical Institute, by then heavily underused and in a rapidly deteriorating area downtown, was sold to the Royal Belfast Academical Institution (Inst), which it abutted, and the proceeds put towards providing rooms for the Ulster Medical Society in the planned new medical building on the Lisburn Road which, in 1976, was christened the Whitla Medical Building. Only a token amount, now unidentifiable, found its way to his former chair, which, since 1967, has been called the Whitla Chair. These eponyms were in recognition of his generosity and prestige rather than strictly on the proceeds of the old Medical Institute's sale, since in 1965 this had realised only £13,052 4s 6d net, of which £500 went to the Royal Victoria Hospital to name a 'Whitla bed'. The taxpayer, via the University Grants Committee, via the university, was ultimately a major source of funds for the modern Ulster Medical Society rooms.[12]

All these professional, intellectual and material achievements, not some momentous discovery or brilliant intellectual triumph, nor some vast USA- or Oxbridge-style endowment (though £8,500 in 1902, and handsome real estate and £35,000 in 1933 were hardly small beer) – *these* were Whitla's legacies to his profession and to

Queen's, while his life and achievements serve as an example to a wider audience of those prepared to learn.

EPILOGUE

As a devout Methodist Whitla would gladly have accepted John Wesley's so-called Rule as an epitaph and in his heart would have considered it truly earned: 'Do all the good you can, by all the means you can, in all the places you can, at all the times you can, as long as ever you can.'

[1] A sixth, Sir Donald Acheson (President 1996–7), formerly Chief Medical Officer, Departments of Health and Social Security, Department of Education and Science and Home Office, 1983–91, was son of an Ulster medical practitioner and brought up in Belfast, but was educated mainly in Britain where he made his career.
[2] J. Cuming, 'The Control of Pathological Research by Clinical Observation', *British Medical Journal* ii (2 August 1884): 201–205.
[3] Peter Froggatt, 'Medicine in Ulster in Relation to the Great Famine and "The Troubles"', *British Medical Journal* 319 (18 December 1999): 1636–1639.
[4] Sir William Whitla, 'The Belfast Medical School: A Survey of the State of Medical Education: Necessary Reforms and the Queen's University of Belfast', *British Medical Journal* ii (31 July 1909): 249–55.
[5] Licentiate of the Royal Colleges of Surgeons and of Physicians of Edinburgh.
[6] See David N. Livingstone, 'Science, Religion and the Geography of Reading: Sir William Whitla and the Editorial Staging of Isaac Newton's Writings on Biblical Prophecy', *British Journal of the History of Science*, 36 (March, 2003): 27–42.
[7] R.G. Shanks, 'The Legacies of Sir William Whitla', *Ulster Medical Journal* 63 (April, 1994): 52–75; see also C.W. Kidd, 'Sir William Whitla, Profile of a Benefactor, *Ulster Medical Journal* 31, no. 1 (1962): 105–116.
[8] The window, to Whitla's own design, had adorned his study in 8 College Square North. In 1902 he gifted it to the Ulster Medical Society for the new Medical Institute, built through his generosity also in College Square North, where it was placed at the top of the staircase. Together with other mementos and artefacts it was transferred in 1976 to the society's new rooms in the aptly named Whitla Medical Building on the Lisburn Road.
[9] Sir William Whitla, *The University Education Question in Ireland: Its Difficulties and their Solution* (Belfast: William Strain, 1899).

10 Quoted from Whitla's speech at his presidential dinner of the Ulster Medical Society on 21 November 1901 when he gave notice of his intention to fund a centre to 'bring the entire local profession under one roof', to be called the Medical Institute, and 'hand it over to Trustees acting on your behalf [provided that] you tell me that you are determined to keep up the building'. (See Shanks, 'The Legacies of Sir William Whitla', 60).

11 See Peter Froggatt, 'The Distinctiveness of Belfast Medicine and its Medical School', *Ulster Medical Journal* 54, no. 2 (1985): 89–108.

12 For the complex negotiations and funding arrangements surrounding these events see Shanks 'The Legacies of Sir William Whitla', 62–5.

James Thomson and the Culture of a Victorian Engineer

PETER J. BOWLER

PETER J. BOWLER is Professor of History of Science at Queen's University.

James Thomson (1822–1892) was the second professor of engineering at Queen's, serving from 1857 to 1873, when he left to take up the chair of engineering at Glasgow. In addition to his teaching he was a practising engineer who made a number of important inventions. He was also active in promoting improvements in the urban environment, especially during his period in Belfast. My title is 'James Thomson and the Culture of a Victorian Engineer', and I want to take that title seriously. I am not a historian of technology, but a historian of science with an interest in evolutionism and the environmental sciences.[1] For help with understanding Thomson's contributions to physics and engineering, I would like to record my thanks to Crosbie Smith and Sir Bernard Crossland. What attracted me to Thomson was the fact that he was much more than an engineer – he was a scientist too, who did important work in physics, but who also related his science (like his engineering) to the natural environment. James Thomson's culture related engineering to natural philosophy in its widest sense, the whole enterprise being driven by his religious beliefs and his social philosophy.

James's brother, William Thomson, later Lord Kelvin, was one of the nineteenth century's most eminent physicists (they were both born in Belfast and Kelvin's statue stands today in the Botanic Gardens). The two collaborated actively in the studies of thermodynamics which made Kelvin's reputation, and James made important studies in other areas of physics bearing on the engineering problems he encountered in the course of his work. Kelvin himself was – as Crosbie Smith has shown – an eminently practical physicist, most of whose work was linked in one way or another to technological developments in areas such as steam power and the electric telegraph.[2] What I want to suggest is that the two brothers stand at opposite ends of a spectrum of interests through which science interacted with technology in the nineteenth century. William was a physicist with a strong interest in engineering, and James was an engineer with a strong interest in physics. They both realised that successful technologies depend on a proper understanding of the physical processes involved. But both also realised that the physics which helps you to understand – and improve – the steam engine or the telegraph also helps you to understand processes going on in the natural world. So Kelvin participated in the great debate over the age of the earth which racked late nineteenth-century geology (and greatly disturbed the Darwinian evolutionists). James studied how flowing water shaped the beds and banks of rivers, how the properties of ice affected the scouring action of glaciers on the landscape, and how the behaviour of the air as a fluid controlled the great wind systems encircling the globe. He was truly an engineer with a broad vision of the world.

The Thomsons were raised as Presbyterians, and both retained a strong religious faith throughout their lives. After much agonising with his conscience, James eventually became a Unitarian. His social views were very much those of a liberal Protestant, exemplifying the best aspects of what has been called the Protestant work ethic. Both brothers expected their involvement in science and engineering to yield benefits to themselves – they were always pleased when an idea was patentable. But at the same time they wanted their inventions to benefit the community as a whole by promoting economic activity or public health. James was active in civic reform, working to benefit the community through the provision of a better water supply, and the creation of public parks where the workers of a newly industrialised city such as Belfast could take the air.

Like many nineteenth-century scientists, both brothers saw their investigations of nature as a means of understanding the divine creation. The motivation underlying their work on thermodynamics was both practical and religious. As Crosbie Smith and M. Norton Wise have shown in their study of Kelvin (cited at note 2), the brothers' world-view focused on the source of energy which drove all natural processes. The ultimate source of energy was God – He had created just so much energy in the beginning, and the laws of nature He had instituted led to an inevitable decline in the amount of energy that was left available for useful work in natural processes. This was a universe with a built-in trend toward what would later be known as the 'heat death', the point at which all matter was at a uniform temperature. At this point the total amount of energy was still the same as at the Creation, but none was available to make anything happen, because useful work can only be obtained if there is a difference of temperature between the source of the energy (such as the steam engine's boiler) and the sink (the environment into which the waste steam and water is exhausted). Small wonder that with a world-view in which the dissipation of useful energy was an inevitable part of the divine plan, the two brothers were driven by a desire to minimise the amount of unnecessary waste in any machine. Throughout their careers, they strove to design machines which extracted as much of the useable energy as possible, losing only what the laws of nature made inevitable.

These views also led them to take up positions on some of the great debates which rocked the scientific world. Kelvin, as is well known, tried to calculate the length of time in which the earth could remain geologically active before cooling to a dead ball of rock. He came up with figures that reduced the amount of geological time to a level at which Darwin's theory of evolution would have been untenable.[3] In the 1860s James wrote to his brother about the relationship between life and the processes of physical nature. He thought that living things might be the only vehicles that could violate the law of the dissipation of useful energy, in effect creating new energy in addition to that supplied to the universe in the Creation.[4] William saw less reason to exempt living things from the laws of physics, suggesting that willpower could only alter the direction of natural processes, switching the consumption of energy into new and unpredictable channels, without actually violating the laws of thermodynamics. It is significant that for both of them the ability of a living body, including that of a human being, to have a real influence on the world was of paramount concern. Science, religion and morality went hand in hand.

Having drawn attention to the richness of the culture within which James Thomson worked, I want to put a little flesh on the bones of the issues I have just sketched in. Let me begin with an outline of his career.[5] He was born in 1822, two years before William. Their father, also James Thomson, was professor of mathematics at the Royal Belfast Academical Institution (Inst). The children were educated at home until their father moved to take up the chair of mathematics at Glasgow in 1834, after which they studied at Glasgow under their father and the other professors.

William eventually went to Cambridge for training in mathematics, while James worked under engineers in various parts of the country, ending up at the Millwall shipbuilding works of William Fairburn, one of the leading figures in the construction of the new ocean-going iron steamships. His health then broke down and he moved back to Glasgow, where he collaborated with William in his work on thermodynamics and began his career as an inventive engineer. In 1851 he moved to Belfast, where he opened an office as a civil engineer and served as engineer to the Water Commissioners. He married Elizabeth Hancock in 1853. The following year he became acting professor of engineering at Queen's, being appointed to the chair of engineering three years later. Thomson replaced James Godwin, the first professor of engineering, who had worked mainly on railways. Although he provided much more teaching than Godwin, Thomson retained his practice as an engineer. He lived for some time at 17 University Square, for which he redesigned the sewers.[6] He remained at Queen's until he took up the chair of engineering at Glasgow in 1873. In 1889 he was forced to resign the chair on account of severe problems with his eyesight – his papers in the archives at Queen's include some letters from this last part of his life written in enormous handwriting, often on very large sheets of paper (although his daughter also acted as his amanuensis).[7] He died in May 1892, followed within a week by his wife and younger daughter, all succumbing to a 'severe cold', probably pneumonia.

While practising as an engineer in Belfast, Thomson served as resident engineer to the Belfast Water Commissioners and advised on the introduction of steam engines to improve the city's water supply. He also designed a weir for the river Lagan. He belonged to many of the societies which served as the backbone of the city's social and intellectual life, and frequently read papers at their meetings. A paper read to the Belfast Social Inquiry Society in 1852 advocated the provision of public parks for the benefit of the citizens, and led indirectly to the creation of the Ormeau Park. Thomson's original preference was for a park much closer to the city centre, created on ground surrounding the Blackstaff river, which he proposed to drain.[8]

Many of Thomson's most important inventions were derived from his studies of fluid motion. In 1850 he patented a vortex turbine which was designed to minimise the loss of energy by careful control of the manner in which the water entered the turbine wheel.[9] High-pressure water was injected from the outside and transferred its energy to specially shaped vanes which kept the water in equilibrium as its pressure dropped. These turbines were immensely successful and were used all over the world. Thomson also designed an improved centrifugal pump which increased efficiency from 50 per cent to 70 per cent and was widely used.[10] He invented a jet pump, which had no moving parts, but relied on a high-pressure jet of water to create a suction effect.[11]

Before he returned to Belfast, James had used his experience with marine steam engines to good effect during the collaboration with his brother which led to the creation of the modern science of thermodynamics. Working from the basic principles of the new science, in 1847 he predicted that the freezing point of water would be decreased if the pressure was increased. This effect was demonstrated experimentally by William in the following year.[12] Arising from this work James became interested in the phenomenon of regelation, by which a wire bearing a load can pass through a block of ice by melting the ice beneath, the water then re-freezing on top of the wire where it is no longer subject to pressure. He read a paper on this phenomenon to the Belfast Natural History and Philosophical Society in 1857 and corresponded with the physicist Michael Faraday on the subject.[13]

Equally significant was his collaboration with Thomas Andrews, his fellow professor at Queen's, who worked during the 1860s on the relationship between liquids and gases. Andrews applied extremely high pressures and low temperatures to gases which had hitherto resisted all efforts to liquefy them. He argued that for these substances there was a continuous change of state, rather than a sharp transition from gas to liquid. Thomson too published extensively in this area.[14]

Thomson's vortex turbine had been inspired by his interest in fluid mechanics, which allowed him to calculate the best way of getting useful work from high-pressure water. As with his work on thermodynamics, a major inspiration was the desire to minimise waste. In a world where energy was, by its very nature, always becoming less available for useful purposes, it was vital that no unnecessary waste should occur. Whether the source was heat in a steam engine, or water-flow in a turbine, the laws of physics could be applied to keep waste to the minimum that nature would allow.

I want to turn now to Thomson's interest in what we would today call the environmental sciences. Although primarily an engineer, his interest in the physics underlying the processes he wished to control encouraged him to study the natural phenomena associated with the areas in which he worked. In a surprising number of cases, this led in turn to original scientific work that was not linked directly to his engineering, but which threw light on the processes which shape our environment – the flow of rivers, the circulation of the winds, and the action of ice on the earth's surface. Thomson's intellectual horizons thus stretched far beyond those that we might expect for someone whose prime enthusiasm was engineering: he was also a natural philosopher in the widest sense of that term – a term still in common use at the start of his career, long before it was replaced by the modern designation of 'scientist'.

As early as 1841, his exploration of the wider implications of the new doctrine of energy led him to speculate about the tides in the oceans. Vast amounts of energy were wasted in the constant rise and fall of the sea level: where did it all come from? By this time the mechanism governing the tides was well understood, but Thomson realised that the rotation of the earth beneath the 'humping' of the seas created by the gravitational pull of the sun and the moon must imply that the seas exert a frictional effect on the planet's rotation. In effect, the tides are gradually slowing down the earth's daily rotation, and that is the source of the energy being dissipated so liberally.[15]

More directly related to his practical work as an engineer for the Belfast Water Commissioners was his interest in the ways in which the water flowing along a river bed actually shapes the course of the river. He investigated the effects of the constant flow of water on the curvature of the river's banks, noting how the land surface would be eroded on the outer part of the curve, while on the inner curve the slackening of the flow would lead to the accumulation of sediment. He even built a model river in which lengths of thread attached to pins could be used to illustrate the direction of flow at different points on the bend.[16] Thomson was able to go far beyond the common-sense understanding of the process by which a river flowing along an alluvial plain tends to increase the size of its loops, eventually leaving some to be isolated as 'ox-bow' lakes. Ever the practical man, he also noted that his insights could be used to explain how the curvature of pipes interfered with the smooth flow of water. Similar arguments were used to explain how some rivers accumulate sand and gravel at their mouths to form 'bars' which block access by shipping.[17]

Thomson's studies of the properties of ice, especially its plasticity under pressure, led him to take an interest in the effects of glaciers in shaping the landscape. Victorian scientists made extensive studies of Alpine glaciers, and the concept of an 'ice age', during which much of northern Europe was covered by ice, was introduced in the 1840s by Louis Agassiz. A number of British geologists were encouraged to explain the topography of the northern parts of the country[18] by assuming that the land was eroded by ice. James Thomson took an interest in a phenomenon which also attracted the attention of the young Charles Darwin: the so-called parallel roads of Lochaber, especially Glen Roy, in Scotland. These horizontal indentations on the upper levels of the valleys were recognised as the remains of ancient beaches, and Darwin hypothesised that they were produced when the whole of Scotland had been sunk beneath the ocean. He later admitted that this was his greatest mistake in science – and it was Thomson who played a major role in establishing the correct explanation. His 1848 paper on the parallel roads of Lochaber argued that the roads were the remains of beaches formed by glacial lakes, created by glaciers damming the lower reaches of the valleys. When the ice melted, the water drained away, leaving the parallel roads to puzzle modern observers.[19]

Thomson's studies of thermodynamics and fluid motion in gases also led him to take an interest in the circulation of winds in the atmosphere. He gave an address to the British Association in Dublin in 1857 in which he used physical principles to explain why the great wind systems of the globe, including the trade winds, circulate in definite bands at particular latitudes.[20] Here he was engaging with another key problem recognised by environmental scientists in the Victorian era, of concern to meteorologists and oceanographers as well as physicists. Thomson's contributions were significant enough for him to be asked to give the Royal Society's Bakerian Lecture on this topic, which was delivered on 10 March 1892, shortly before his death.[21] Interestingly, Thomson's papers in the Queen's University archives also show that he was trying to apply the same principles to explain the coloured bands on the surface of the planet Jupiter. He was forced to admit, however, that his theory would not work, given the astronomers' arguments that Jupiter's atmosphere is immensely deep. His ideas *would* apply, he insisted, to a Jupiter-sized planet with a thin atmosphere like the earth's.[22]

I will conclude with another of Thomson's contributions to the environmental sciences, one with a particular local flavour. In 1877 he published a paper on the forces that could have produced the unusual columnar structures found at the Giant's Causeway. It was widely admitted by then that basaltic rocks had cooled from a molten state, but geologists were puzzled as to the nature of the forces that could build up in the solidifying rock to produce such regular fractures. Some thought the sections of the columns had begun as spheres of solidifying rock which expanded until they intersected with one another. Thomson rejected this view and supported a rival theory in which forces analogous to those which create the cracks in drying mud were responsible, but he was able to provide a much more detailed account of the way the forces would build up within a deep, homogeneous mass of cooling rock.[23]

I hope that I have given enough examples to show that James Thomson was not only an engineer of genius but also a scientist who thought on the grandest possible scale about the physical forces which governed the processes he wished to control. He was not content to study those forces solely on the small scale needed to design pumps and turbines – he was fascinated by the way the same forces operated on a global scale to create major features of our environment. Given his interest in public health, and the supply of clean water and of open spaces within the city, we can see him as a figure whose work not only helped bring together the activities of the scientist and the engineer, but who also saw both science and technology as operating within a global system which it was our duty to understand with a view to benefiting the whole of humankind. If this was the culture of a Victorian engineer, it was a culture with the widest possible dimensions.

1   See, for instance, Peter J. Bowler, *The Fontana History of the Environmental Sciences* (London: Fontana, 1992), which provides background on some of the issues discussed below.
2   See Crosbie Smith and M. Norton Wise, *Energy and Empire: A Biographical Study of Lord Kelvin* (Cambridge: Cambridge University Press, 1989). This book also contains a wealth of information on James Thomson.
3   In addition to the discussions in Smith and Wise, *Energy and Empire*, see also Joe D. Burchfield, *Lord Kelvin and the Age of the Earth* (New York: Science History Publications, 1975).
4   James Thomson to William Thomson, 7 April 1862, quoted in *Collected Papers on Physics and Engineering by James Thomson*, ed. Sir Joseph Larmor and James Thomson (Cambridge: Cambridge University Press, 1912), lv–lvii, and William's reply of 21 April 1862, ibid., lvii–lviii.
5   On Thomson's career, see the 'Biographical Sketch' in *Collected Papers*, xiii–xci, and the 'Obituary Notice' by J. T. Bottomley, reprinted from the *Proceedings of the Royal Society*, 1893, in *Collected Papers*, xcii–cii; Crosbie Smith, 'James Thomson', *The Oxford Dictionary of National Biography*, vol. 54, 527–7. See also Bernard Crossland, 'James Thomson', in *The Lives of the Great Engineers of Ulster: Vol. 1*, eds. Crossland and John S. Moore (Belfast: NE Consultancy for Belfast Industrial Heritage, 2003), 149–56. I am grateful to Sir Bernard for sending me a copy of the proof of this article in advance of publication.
6   See the drawings of September 1866 held in Queen's University Library, Thomson Papers MS13, section L, item 5.
7   See, for instance, James Thomson to William Thomson, 21 September 1891, Thomson Papers, MS13, section H.
8   James Thomson, 'On Public Parks in Connection with Large Towns, with a Suggestion for the Formation of a Park in Belfast', reprinted in *Collected Papers*, 464–72.
9   See Thomson's account to the British Association for the Advancement of Science, 1852, 'On the Vortex Water Wheel', reprinted in *Collected Papers*, 2–16.
10 James Thomson, 'On a Centrifugal Pump with Exterior Whirlpool, Constructed for Draining Land', reprinted from *Proceedings of the Engineers of Scotland*, 1858, in *Collected Papers*, 16–24.
11 James Thomson, 'On a Jet Pump, an Apparatus for Drawing Up Water by the Power of a Jet', reprinted from the report of the British Association for the Advancement of Science, 1852, in *Collected Papers*, 26–7.
12 James Thomson, 'Theoretical Considerations on the Effect of Pressure in Lowering the Freezing Point of Water', reprinted from *The Cambridge and Dublin Mathematical Journal*, 1850, in *Collected Papers*, 196–203, and William Thomson, 'The Effect of Pressure in Lowering the Freezing Point of Water Experimentally Demonstrated', reprinted from *Proceedings of the Royal Society of Edinburgh*, 1850, in *Collected Papers*, 204–8.
13 There is a copy of the report of the paper to the Belfast Natural History and

Philosophical Society, with a later note dated 1866, in Queen's University Library, Thomson Papers, section I, item 1. See also Thomson, 'On the Plasticity of Ice, as Manifested in Glaciers', reprinted from *Proceedings of the Royal Society*, 1856–57, in *Collected Papers*, 208–11, and the letters between Thomson and Faraday, *Collected Papers*, 212–19.

[14] A number of papers on the topic are reprinted in *Collected Papers*, 276–333. There are also many items on the topic in Queen's University Library, Thomson Papers, section J. See J.S. Rowlinson, 'The Work of Thomas Andrews and James Thomson on the Liquefaction of Gases', *Notes and Records of the Royal Society of London* 57 (2003): 143–59. I am grateful to Professor Rowlinson for supplying me with a copy of his paper.

[15] See James Thomson's letter of 9 July 1862 to William, quoted in Smith and Wise, *Energy and Empire,* 285 (original in the Kelvin Collection, University of Glasgow).

[16] James Thomson, 'Experimental Demonstration in respect to the Origin of the Windings of Rivers in Alluvial Plains', reprinted from *Proceedings of the Royal Society*, 1873, in *Collected Papers*, 100–1, and numerous other papers on this topic reprinted in the same volume.

[17] See the notes for papers dated 1887–9, Queen's University Library, Thomson Papers, section E.

[18] The glaciation was mostly in Scotland but extended to other parts including north Wales, and parts of Ireland.

[19] James Thomson, 'On the Parallel Roads of Lochaber', reprinted from the *Edinburgh New Philosophical Journal,* 1848, in *Collected Papers*, 407–20. See Martin J.S. Rudwick, 'Darwin and Glen Roy: A "Great Failure" in Scientific Method?', *Studies in the History and Philosophy of Science* 5 (1974): 97–185.

[20] As far as I know the 1857 lecture was never printed. All we know of it is the reference in the later paper cited here.

[21] James Thomson, 'Bakerian Lecture : On the Great Currents of Atmospheric Circulation', reprinted from *Philosophical Transactions of the Royal Society,* 1892, in *Collected Papers*, 153–95; on the 1857 address, see 182.

[22] Queen's University Library, Thomson Papers, section H.

[23] James Thomson, 'On the Jointed Prismatic Structure in Basaltic Rocks', reprinted from *Transactions of the Geological Society of Glasgow*, 1877, in *Collected Papers,* 422–40.

Helen Waddell
and Literary Europe

NORMAN VANCE

NORMAN VANCE is Professor of English at the University of Sussex.

Helen Waddell (1889–1965), poet and translator, pioneering medievalist, historical novelist and dramatist, is the most distinguished and celebrated writer to have been associated with Queen's University Belfast in its Edwardian infancy, albeit only as a student at the time.[1] She passed the matriculation exams in 1907, was awarded a First in English in 1911, one of just three candidates for the new honours degree, and earned an MA in English the following year for a thesis on Milton. But her writing and her imagination, further stimulated by subsequent study in Oxford and Paris, encompassed not just the Englishness of English literature but a timeless vision of 'Literary Europe' from Boethius to Baudelaire, indeed from Virgil and Petronius Arbiter to Thomas Hardy and William Butler Yeats.[2]

Perhaps four factors contributed to this range and emphasis: her non-European childhood as a missionary's daughter in Japan, her broadly based studies at Queen's, the new hopes for Europe after the First World War, and the looming despair of Europe in crisis in the darkest days of the Second World War.

The Japanese experience, which was unlike anything else in her life, gave her a unique vantage point from which to see Europe steadily and see it whole. Her father, originally a missionary in China before going to Japan, had been involved in the work of biblical translation into Japanese, and in 1913 she herself published a brilliant collection of *Lyrics from the Chinese*, selected and adapted from a published collection of prose translations belonging to her father.[3] If, as I have argued elsewhere, the translator's moral and religious imagination could span continents and widely diverse cultures and find the terms to communicate universal truths and perceptions, it could certainly seek and find common meanings in the different languages and experiences of Christian Europe after the fall of Rome.[4]

Childhood and life in Japan did not last. Waddell's mother had died early, and then her father died. She moved to Belfast when she was twelve, with her sister and her stepmother, and went to Victoria College. Perhaps it is not too fanciful to suggest that her romantic fascination with the vigorously imagined life of English and European literature was a kind of substitute for lost parents and an irrecoverably lost exotic childhood. She certainly claimed that at the age of twelve she was moved by a kind of homesickness, 'what some writers call the "nostalgie de l'infini"', and this found expression in an emotional as well as religious fascination with the opening words of St Augustine's *Confessions*: *Fecisti nos ad te* ... 'Thou hast made us for thyself, and our hearts are restless until they find rest in Thee.'[5]

Waddell was so much a restless romantic that it is rather startling to learn that she might have been a Queen's mathematician. After matriculating as a student of the old Royal University of Ireland in 1907, she was persuaded with some difficulty to wait for a year and have some additional maths coaching to prepare for an entrance scholarship. She was so well coached and had such natural ability that she not only won the much-needed scholarship but was awarded second-class honours in Maths in First Arts in 1909. By then the Queen's College had become the Queen's University and from July 1909 there was a new degree structure, with the new possibility in the arts faculty of a specialised honours degree in a single discipline such as maths or English or classics. Professor A.C. Dixon wanted her for the new honours school of maths, Professor R.M. Henry had made her read in the honours Latin class in her first year, and Professor Gregory Smith needed her for the new honours school of English. Smith, or 'Gregory the Great' as Helen Waddell was to call him, was the winner. But First Arts, like matriculation, involved everyone in a wide range of studies: not just compulsory maths, Latin, English and natural philosophy but French or some other language as well. Most aspired just to pass First Arts, but classified honours could be awarded for individual subjects, and Helen Waddell won first class honours in English and French and second class honours in Latin in addition to her success in maths. She then took further courses in French and Latin since two subsidiary subjects were required as part of the requirements for the single honours degree in English.[6] Well-taught both at Victoria College and at Queen's, she learnt enough French and Latin alongside her English studies to become a serious student, and later professional translator, of French and Latin literature.

In any case, university English, at this time a fairly new discipline often directed by well-read Oxford classicists, positively encouraged breadth of interest. Gregory Smith, one of the many talented Scots who had completed his education at Balliol, and recently arrived at Queen's from teaching in the English department at Edinburgh, was initially professor of both history and English. He had already demonstrated historical as well as literary learning by publishing in both fields, and he had a strong interest in other European literatures and in Scottish writing.[7] In 1900 he had contributed a very scholarly volume on the later Middle Ages (unimaginatively entitled *The Transition Period*) to an outstanding new series on the Periods of European Literature. This was under the general editorship of his old Edinburgh professor George Saintsbury.[8] Saintsbury, an Oxford classicist and Merton man, later Helen Waddell's external examiner for both her BA and her MA, was to become her most faithful mentor and friend. As a young man he had lived in the Channel Islands and published widely on French as well as English literature, writing one of the first appreciations of Baudelaire in English. The epigraph he chose for the Periods of European Literature series was taken from a famous essay on 'The Function of Criticism' (1864) by that literary cosmopolitan Matthew Arnold, also an Oxford classicist, and another Balliol man like Gregory Smith:

> The criticism which alone can much help us for the future is a criticism which regards Europe as being, for intellectual and spiritual purposes, one great confederation, bound to a joint action and working to a common result.[9]

It was very much in this spirit that Helen Waddell, as a research student at Somerville College Oxford (where her friend from Queen's Maud Clarke was now teaching history), gave some Advanced Studies lectures in 1921 on 'Mime in the Middle Ages'. She began the series by announcing boldly that 'French, Italian and Spanish are provincial dialects, not of Gothic, the language of the conquerors, but of Latin, the language of the conquered'.[10] Though the focus of her medieval research shifted from drama to lyric, and then from the influence of the Latin lyric on vernacular European literature to the Latin lyric itself,[11] she continued to be fascinated with the pan-European dimension of Latin culture and with the long shadow cast by the Latin language and Latin culture despite the fall of Rome and military defeat by Ostrogoths and Visigoths.

It all seemed finally to come to an end in August 1914. The catastrophe of the war in Europe from 1914 to 1918 seriously damaged older Romantic visions of the cultural and spiritual unity of Europe, dreams of the kind celebrated by Matthew Arnold and the German Romantic Novalis (Friedrich von Hardenberg) in his essay *Christianity or Europe* (written 1799). The new bitterness in Europe, particularly between France and Germany, continued into the 1920s, but the mutual guarantee of Franco–German and Belgian–German frontiers in the Locarno Pact of 1925 did something to relieve international tension and produced a fairly short-lived atmosphere of optimism which continued when Germany was admitted to the League of Nations in 1926.[12] It was against this background, 'when the peace was not half a decade old and Locarno shone over Europe like a harvest moon', as she rather fancifully put it,[13] that Helen Waddell began to write up what she had found out about medieval lyric and the medieval scholars who wrote it. *The Wandering Scholars* was finished at the end of 1926 and published in 1927, and her first collection of *Medieval Latin Lyrics* came out in 1929. Her medieval novel *Peter Abelard*, based on the ill-fated love-story of Abelard, the Paris theologian, and Heloise, appeared in 1933.

All three books were spectacularly successful, admired by peers and prime ministers, notably Ramsay MacDonald, and ran through many editions, making available to a popular readership materials which had previously been the preserve of academic specialists. Some of the experts, not untouched by professional jealousy, were to grumble that Waddell's selection of literary material was unrepresentative. Perhaps in reaction against her Presbyterian nurture, she had cheerfully over-emphasised drinking songs such as the *Confessio* of the twelfth-century Archpoet who had insisted that

> Meum est propositum
> in taberna mori,
> ut sint vina proxima
> morientis ori.

She translated this, with impressive tonal and metrical faithfulness, as

> For on this my heart is set:
> When the hour is nigh me,
> Let me in the tavern die,
> With a tankard by me.[14]

Waddell also celebrated unofficial exuberance such as that found in the thirteenth-century *Carmina Burana*, preserved in a Bavarian monastery, not yet very satisfactorily edited, nor made famous to generations of singers by the musical settings of Carl Orff. The critics complained in particular that she had not translated some of the gravest and greatest verse in medieval Latin. Her reply was that they were quite right: she had tried to but simply could not, adding that a translator could not make a translation happen to order any more than a poet could produce a poem to order.[15]

This high-Romantic view of the task of the verse translator as a creative art not only licensed personal preferences but also allowed her to select, and project, an apparently timeless and ageless, optimistically humanistic tradition of European lyric, favouring the more interesting and vivid secular poets who seemed to her to have 'kept the imagination of Europe alive'.[16] The common concerns of her chosen poets, and indeed her formidable assembly of secondary authorities – English, French, German, occasionally Italian – in a sense represented a literary version of much-desired European, and more specifically Franco-German, accord. The British Library, the Bibliothèque Nationale in Paris and the Monastery of Benedictbeuern in Bavaria were the resting places of much of her material, which belonged to the whole of Europe. It was not always clear precisely which country could claim particular poems, but it hardly mattered. In one of her reports from Paris she notes with wry amusement that since much of her material was anonymous 'this problem of authorship and national jealousy has been a bone of contention among German scholars since 1807' and that she felt it was more important 'to postpone the questions of authorship and provenance, and get to work on the stuff itself'.[17] To oversimplify, a kind of involuntary Franco-German cooperation, mainly the combination of French taste and German scholarship, was the foundation of her work. She also made good use of the work based on French sources of contemporary French scholars such as Joseph Bédier and

Edmond Faral, whom she had originally proposed as her research supervisors in Paris.[18] But before them, before the Great War had changed everything, there had been the late-Romantic fascination in France with decadent Rome and the medieval Latin literature which released the language and its verse forms from the straitjacket of formal classicism. Charles Baudelaire's *Les Fleurs du Mal* (1857) had included a poem in Latin ('Franciscae meae laudes'), closely modelled on the rhythm and verse structure of that great medieval hymn *Dies Irae*.[19] Rémy de Gourmont, essayist and critic, one of the founders of the leading Symboliste journal *Mercure de France*, had published a study of *Le Latin Mystique* in 1890: the edition of 1922 also featured in the text as well as the bibliography of Helen Waddell's *The Wandering Scholars*. One of the main sources for curious French Romantics and decadents, Edelstand Du Méril's *Poésies Populaires Latines du Moyen Âge* (1847), was one of her sources too.[20] The English antiquary Thomas Wright had published editions of medieval Latin poetry since the 1830s. There was an edition of sorts of the *Carmina Burana* by the German Johan Andreas Schmeller, published in Stuttgart in 1847, and there were dusty standard compilations such as Migne's still indispensable though indigestible *Patrologia Latina*, published in Paris from 1844, and the four volumes of *Poetae Latini Carolini Aevi* published in Berlin from 1881 to 1923. What is remarkable, however, is not this League of Nations of dry and often elderly scholarship, some of it originally available to her in Belfast, in the Queen's Library, so much as the fresh and yet somehow timeless universal poetic vision which could be unlocked from it by the right sort of imaginative reader. To take just one example, 'De ramis cadunt folia', an early thirteenth-century poem about autumn and winter collected eighty years before by Du Méril, comes to life in Waddell's hands:

> Down from the branches fall the leaves,
> A wanness comes on all the trees,
> The summer's done;
> And into his last house in heaven
> Now goes the sun.[21]

It may have been the Locarno spirit of international cooperation that turned Helen Waddell towards the eighteenth-century French novelist Abbé Prévost, literary hack in Paris, Amsterdam and London, author of *Manon Lescaut* (1731) and French translator of the novels of Samuel Richardson. It may also have been her more general interest in eighteenth-century literature, which had been encouraged by her mentors Gregory Smith and George Saintsbury as good for her prose style. Prévost was attractive to her as a novelist of powerful feeling and a literary personality, someone whose practical incompetence, simplicity and susceptibility to goodness she associated with that of Goldsmith. He was also of interest as a journalist who founded a magazine, *Le Pour et Contre*, intended to teach the French more about English culture and vice versa. In 1931, to mark the two hundredth anniversary of *Manon Lescaut*, she translated it into terse, syntactically elegant English, which is both idiomatic and surprisingly literal and compares very favourably with the simpler but flatter English of the subsequent Penguin translation.[22] This close encounter with the novel, which draws on Prévost's own experiences in an often difficult life, encouraged her to write a well-made play about Prévost which would dramatise and tease out the possible autobiographical connections. Her brother Samuel, also known as the dramatist Rutherford Mayne of the Ulster Literary Theatre, and Sam's friend Lennox Robinson, the Irish dramatist and theatre manager, were interested in the project and took a careful professional look at it for her. A key phrase in *Manon Lescaut* is *Je la perdis*, 'I lost her', the protagonist's cry of anguish as he recalls how his wayward beloved died in his arms. It is also the last line of the play, as the Prévost character recalls the death of the love of his life, the worthless Lenki.[23]

Later, in a very different Europe after the fall of France, Helen Waddell translated and published her friend Guy Robin's patriotic tract *A French Soldier Speaks* (1941).[24] She described Robin, a desperately wounded French soldier who had escaped to London, as 'a young man whose spiritual ancestry dates from Roncesvalles', when, according to the poetic legend of the *Chanson de Roland*, the Moors were repelled from Charlemagne's France. Like Robin, she had a profound sense of the now imperilled civilization of Christian Europe occupied by Nazi Germany. With this, for him and for her, there went a new sense of kinship with the Roman struggle against encroaching barbarism.[25] This distracted her from her current work on the Englishman John of Salisbury and in April 1940 she turned instead to read and translate from Virgil, poet of the moment of catastrophe and the prospect of renewal, of the fall of Troy, *fuit Ilium* ('It might be yesterday,' she wrote), and of the eventual triumph of Rome.[26] She began to think again about the long history of Latin poetry after Virgil which carried forward into the Middle Ages the Roman, and eventually the European, tradition of civility and of Christian witness. There was consolation to be found in the lines of the poet Arator, who in the sixth century had proclaimed the eternity of the Christian faith of Rome in time of war, during the Lombard occupation. Using the inherited metre and vocabulary of Virgil, who had sung of the walls of lofty Rome, he insisted that

> these solemn walls
> Shall stand, shaken, it may be, not destroyed
> By any trampling of the hosts of hate.
> That road is closed to war, whose gate
> Stands open to the stars.

Helen Waddell inscribed her translation of these lines 'For Vilpuri, Cracow, Prague'.[27]

When Guy Robin died in August 1941 she was profoundly upset but found some relief in translating Alcuin's eighth-century poem to St Michael, also written in wartime:

> O Michael, servant of the eternal King,
> Standing upon the citadel of Heaven ...
> Cease not to help thy feeble folk,
> Until the struggle of this war is spent.[28]

Alcuin, a Yorkshireman before he became a famous scholar and teacher at the court of Charlemagne, had known deep distress as the Vikings attacked Lindisfarne. As the bombers flew over the ruins of Lindisfarne in the 1940s, his wide-ranging reflections took on a newly topical significance, pointing another more sceptical age to the eternal glory which lies beyond looming temporal disaster. Mighty Babylon, Persia, the empire of Alexander, Rome and Jerusalem themselves had come to know ruin and destruction, but at the end of a long meditation on the ravages of war and the deeds of the wicked, Alcuin concludes with a joyful doxology, ascribing to God (in the Waddell translation)

> praise and worship, honour, strength,
> A blessing and a song, for evermore.[29]

Some of the new translations produced under the pressure and distress of war (from which she never really recovered) were incorporated in her W.P. Ker Lecture on *Poetry in the Dark Ages* in 1947, almost her last published work. This paid tribute to Ker's book *The Dark Ages* (1904), the first volume of that formidable series on Periods of European Literature to which her mentors Gregory Smith and George Saintsbury had contributed.[30] Twenty-five years previously, she said, Ker's book had introduced her to Boethius, called the last of the Romans, philosopher, poet and author of *The Consolation of Philosophy*, which was written when he was the prisoner of Theodoric the Ostrogoth (*c.* 524). Boethius in his cell had become for her the type of wartime prisoners in Dachau. But Boethius in his extremity had found comfort in poetry and prayer to the eternal creator of the starry heavens, the timeless source of life and light and father of all men:

> There is no race of men
> But rose from one same spring.
> One father of them all,
> To all things giving.
> He gave the sun his beams
> The moon her crescent of light,
> To earth he gave mankind,
> Stars to the night.[31]

Helen Waddell shared this timeless literary and religious vision, intensified by the particular stresses of war and historical crisis, yet ultimately transhistorical and transcultural. This was the vision that allowed her in imagination to rejoice with the wandering scholars of Europe, to share the love and the pain of Abelard and Heloise and Manon Lescaut, and to see hope beyond a Europe in ruins. Queen's University Belfast, and all of us, should honour her.

1. See Monica Blackett, *The Mark of the Maker: A Portrait of Helen Waddell* (London: Constable, 1973), and Felicitas Corrigan, *Helen Waddell: A Biography* (London: Gollancz, 1986); for critical commentary, see Jennifer Fitzgerald, '"Jazzing the Middle Ages": The Feminist Genesis of Helen Waddell's *The Wandering Scholars*', *Irish Studies Review* 8, no. 1 (April 2000): 5–22, and 'Truth's Martyr or Love's Martyr: Helen Waddell's *Peter Abelard*', *Colby Quarterly* 36, no. 2 (June 2000): 176–87; see also David Burleigh, 'The Early Writings of Helen Waddell on Japan: A Survey and Interpretation' (MPhil thesis, University of Sussex, 2000) and David Burleigh (ed.), *Helen Waddell's Writings from Japan* (Dublin: Irish Academic Press, 2005).
2. For Waddell's interest in Baudelaire, see Joanna Richardson, *Enid Starkie* (London: John Murray, 1973), 102; there are passing references to Hardy (also to Marlowe and Keats, Ronsard and Du Bellay, John Gay's *The Beggar's Opera*, and the criticism of Walter Pater) in Waddell's *The Wandering Scholars* (1927; revised edition, London: Constable, 1934), 18, 21, 43, 129; there is an enigmatic passing reference to Yeats in a notebook mainly concerned with medieval and renaissance literature, Queen's University Belfast (QUB) Waddell Papers MS 18/1(d), 1.
3. Helen Waddell, *Lyrics from the Chinese* (London: Constable, 1913), based on James Legge, tr., *The Shee King, or Book of Poetry*, The Chinese Classics, vol. 4, pt 1 (Hong Kong: 1871, reprinted Hong Kong: Hong Kong University Press, 1960). Unless otherwise indicated, all subsequent works of Helen Waddell were also first published by Constable.
4. See Norman Vance, *Helen Waddell: Presbyterian Medievalist* (Belfast: Presbyterian Historical Society, 1997), 10, 18.
5. Corrigan, *Helen Waddell*, 58–9.
6. Ibid., 73; T.W. Moody and J.C. Beckett, *Queen's, Belfast, 1845–1949: The History of a University*, 2 vols (London: Faber & Faber, 1959), 1:418–22; *QUB Calendar, 1910*, 501–2.
7. On Gregory Smith and the history of English at Queen's, see Edna Longley, '"A Foreign Oasis"?: English Literature, Irish Studies and Queen's University Belfast', *Irish Studies Review* 17/18 (Winter, 1995): 26–39.
8. Ranging from W.P. Ker's *The Dark Ages* to George Saintsbury's *The Later Nineteenth Century*, the series was completed in 12 volumes (Edinburgh: William Blackwood & Sons, 1897–1907).
9. Matthew Arnold, 'The Function of Criticism at the Present Time', in Arnold, *Essays in Criticism*, 1st ser., (1865; reprint, London: Dent, 1964), 33.
10. Corrigan, *Helen Waddell*, 203.
11. See Helen Waddell to Miss Grier, Lady Margaret Hall (LMH), Oxford, 12 January 1924, seeking renewal of the Susette Taylor Travelling Fellowship to which the College (LMH) had elected her (LMH Archives). I am very grateful to Julie Courtenay, LMH Archivist, for copies of this document and of the material referred to in notes 17 and 18 below.
12. For a contemporary view of the international relations of the period, as they were perceived and discussed at Queen's and elsewhere, see W.G. Moore, *France and Germany: An Introduction to a European Problem* (London:

SCM Press, 1932), inscribed 'In Memory of all victims of the Great War'. My father, William Vance, bought and read this book while a student at QUB in the early 1930s.
13. Helen Waddell, *More Latin Lyrics: From Virgil to Milton*, ed. Felicitas Corrigan (London: Gollancz, 1976), 36.
14. Helen Waddell, *Medieval Latin Lyrics* (1929), (Harmondsworth: Penguin Books, 1952), 188-9.
15. Waddell, *Medieval Latin Lyrics*, 8.
16. Waddell, *Wandering Scholars*, 220.
17. Helen Waddell to The Principal, Lady Margaret Hall, Oxford, 26 February 1924 (LMH Archives).
18. Helen Waddell to The Principal, Lady Margaret Hall, 30 April 1923 (original application for the Susette Taylor Fellowship which allowed her to study in Paris, LMH Archives).
19. It should be noted that it was through Helen Waddell's critical interest and good offices that her fellow Somervillian Enid Starkie's pioneering study of Baudelaire was published in 1933. See Richardson, *Enid Starkie*, 102.
20. Rémy de Gourmont, *Le Latin Mystique* (Paris: Cres, 1922); Edelstand Du Méril, *Poésies Populaires Latines du Moyen Âge* (Paris: Firmin Didot Frères, 1847).
21. Waddell, *Medieval Latin Lyrics*, 286–7.
22. An unused MS draft of the Translator's Note for Waddell's translation reads 'For the bi-centenary of the first printing of Manon Lescaut at Amsterdam in 1731': QUB Waddell Papers, MS 18/7; Compare *Manon Lescaut*, tr. L.W. Tancock (Harmondsworth: Penguin Books, 1949).
23. Helen Waddell, *The Abbé Prévost: A Play* (London: Constable, 1933), 59. Holograph MS in QUB Waddell Papers, MS 18/6. The play was performed, but not altogether satisfactorily; the interest and promised help of George Bernard Shaw came to nothing.
24. Guy Robin, *A French Soldier Speaks*, tr. Helen Waddell (London: Constable, 1941).
25. Robin, *A French Soldier Speaks*, iii, 65, 68, 77.
26. Virgil, *Aeneid* II, 325; Blackett, 149 quotes a letter of April 1940: 'I have been so haunted by France that I went back to Virgil, the fall of Troy, and all the old Fifth Column business of the Trojan Horse ...'.
27. Helen Waddell, *More Latin Lyrics*, 157. Waddell refers to this poem as 'a forgotten memory of Alcuin' (ibid., 36) but it is actually by Arator, revised by Alcuin. Arator's word for the strong walls of Rome, *moenia*, is the one used by Virgil at the beginning of the *Aeneid* (I, 7) as he looks forward to the eventual foundation of Rome.
28. Corrigan, *Helen Waddell*, 314; Latin text in Migne PL (*Patrologia Latina*, 101 col. 770 no. 168), and full text of translation in *More Latin Lyrics*, 179.
29. Alcuin, 'De rerum humanarum vicissitudine et clade Lindisfarnensis monasterii' (Migne PL, 101 cols 805–10); translation in *More Latin Lyrics*, 175.

30 Helen Waddell, *Poetry in the Dark Ages* (Glasgow: Jackson, 1948); W.P. Ker, *The Dark Ages* (Edinburgh: William Blackwood, 1904).
31 Boethius, *De Consolatione Philosophiae* III, 6, translated in *More Latin Lyrics*, 109; see also Boethius, I, 5, *More Latin Lyrics*, 97.

Maurice Powicke

Medieval Historical Scholarship and Queen's

MAURICE KEEN

MAURICE KEEN is Emeritus Fellow of Balliol College, Oxford.

My title, 'Maurice Powicke: Medieval Historical Scholarship and Queen's', defines an assignment that proved more problematic than it looks. The facts fit together far less easily than they ought to. Frederick Maurice Powicke (1879–1963) was in 1909 appointed to be the first professor of modern history at Queen's University: there had been no separate chair of history in the former Queen's College. He held the chair until 1919. After that he lived to be generally recognised, in the mid-twentieth century, as the most powerful personal influence in British medieval studies of his generation. From that same twentieth century, the tally of illustrious names in medieval historical scholarship that have an association with Queen's is a profoundly impressive one: Maud Clarke, Harold Cronne, R.R. Betts, D.B. Quinn, Jack Gray, Michael Dolley, Art Cosgrove and, last and most of all, the late Lewis Warren. Clearly there ought to be a connection between, on the one hand, Powicke's early tenure of the chair and his tremendous influence in the field and, on the other, the undoubted distinction of Queen's, its staff and alumni in the same field of medieval history. But when one starts to search it proves extraordinarily hard to pin down any such a connection. I will try to get round this problem by initially separating the two themes, talking first of Powicke, then of Queen's and medieval studies, coming back at the end to see if there is any way of bridging the surprising gap between the two stories.

Powicke was born at Alnwick, County Northumberland in 1879, the eldest son of a Congregational minister. His schooling was at Stockport Grammar School, from where he went on, in 1896, to study history at Manchester University under the great T.F. Tout, who for many years to come would be his chief patron, guide, philosopher and true friend. From Manchester he proceeded to Oxford, to Tout's old College, Balliol, where A.L. Smith and H.W.C. Davis were among his teachers. He was disappointed by a second class honours in 'Greats' (classical history and philosophy) in 1902, but achieved a first in history after only a year's further study in 1903. After that he was briefly a research fellow of Merton

College, then an assistant lecturer at Liverpool; he was rescued by Tout from the near catastrophe of non-renewal at Liverpool with an assistant lectureship at Manchester. Tout's influence again helped him toward a second term of research fellowship at Merton in 1908. Thence he came, a year later, to the chair at Queen's. In 1919, when Tout retired from his Manchester professorship, Powicke was elected to succeed him, and nine years after that, in 1928, he was named to succeed another of his teachers, H.W.C. Davis, as Regius professor of history at Oxford, with a fellowship at Oriel College. In 1946, the year before he retired, he was knighted for his services to history. Oxford remained his home till his death in 1963. He was much loved and revered there; all three of the colleges with which he had had association – Oriel, Merton and Balliol – elected him to honorary fellowships. In my very early days as a young fellow of Balliol I remember him coming into the college regularly, a tiny, white-haired, white-moustached figure, crossing the quadrangle in his dark overcoat, his black homburg hat, and with an unrolled umbrella. He had a gentle voice and a very kind smile, and was so short that when he sat in one of the high armchairs in the Senior Common Room to take his coffee, one noticed that his feet did not quite touch the ground.

Tout in his time as professor had made Manchester the foremost centre of medieval historical research in Britain. Powicke as his successor maintained this tradition, and brought thence to Oxford the standards and professional commitment to research scholarship that had been the pride of the Manchester School. Over his years as Regius professor that tradition, transplanted, together with his personal energy and charisma, brought Oxford to pre-eminence in the field. He was the real founder of postgraduate study in the history school there, the first to teach the tutors of Oxford to take seriously the new graduate degrees, the doctorate and the BLitt, offering a shining example himself of conscientious commitment and pastoral care as a graduate supervisor. Some older Oxford tutors mocked as the 'Powickery' his Medieval Group, the band of younger college fellows and research students whom he gathered to informal meetings in his Oriel rooms, to hear papers and discuss research problems. The names of some of those who were among his regulars give the lie to the jeering: Richard Southern, Beryl Smalley,

Richard Hunt, Christopher Cheney – names among the greatest English medieval scholars of the next generation.

As Oxford's Regius professor Powicke was naturally a force in the academic world beyond his university as well as within it. He was a fellow of the British Academy from 1927, and from 1933 to 1937 he was president of the Royal Historical Society. It was typical of him that his first presidential address should have been entitled 'Modern Methods of Medieval Research', and that its burden was to urge the development of major collaborative research enterprises. The efforts in cooperation that he sought to foster were not all equally successful; but his project for a new and enlarged version of Wilkin's *Concilia* – the records of medieval British Church councils – proved ultimately a triumph, its direction carried forward by the diligence first of Christopher Cheney and after him of Christopher Brooke. The third and final volume of *Councils and Synods*, as it was now entitled, appeared in 1981 (3 vols, Oxford, Clarendon Press, 1932, 1964, 1981). Throughout his career Powicke was a prolific author of books, articles and reviews. Four major books are now the best remembered of his works: *The Loss of Normandy* (Manchester University Press, 1913), *Stephen Langton* (Oxford, Clarendon Press, 1928), *King Henry III and the Lord Edward* (Oxford, Clarendon Press, 1947), and *The Thirteenth Century* (Oxford, Clarendon Press, 1953). They share distinctive common characteristics. Political narrative and its institutional background offered the framework with which Powicke was most at ease. His reconstructions bore the mark of his meticulous scholarship – his footnotes were often long. His care with his choice of words and his elegant literary style expressed evocatively the sensitivities and sensibilities of his very personal perceptions: his insights into the complexities of human character, his feeling for the atmospherics of places and buildings, his alertness to the ways in which political development and the history of ideas can interact. He had a very keen eye for vivid and telling detail, and enjoyed lingering over subjects and scenes that had engrossed him imaginatively. His books tend in consequence to be slow moving, stronger on description and reconstruction than on analysis. *King Henry III and the Lord Edward*, the magnum opus of his own estimation, has been described, justly but in a not unreservedly flattering spirit, as Proustian. He never wrote and would never have wished to write in a way that would meet the needs of the hurried student, and for our generally more hurried age his style of historical writing is no longer easy to respond to.

Powicke's most original and important contribution to historical thinking was his perception of the relevance of the study of the intellectual developments of the schools to the study of political development in the medieval period. His work for his book on Stephen Langton, the scholar bishop who was such an important actor in the events leading up to the Magna Carta, was what first awakened him to the importance of their interplay. Because he himself remained better attuned personally to the exploration of character than of concepts, the full potential of his insight was never quite realised in his own writing, but it left a very powerful mark on the young scholars of the next generation who came under his influence, most notably Richard Southern.

The Loss of Normandy, Powicke's first book and probably the most sharply written and most often read among them, was the principal publication of his years at Queen's. Of those years, I would say that it seems easier to assess what Queen's did for Powicke that what Powicke did for Queen's. Before he came to Queen's he had been often assailed by lack of confidence and had craved a security that eluded him. At Oxford he had been disappointed by his second in Greats; by coming only *proxime* in the coveted Stanhope Historical Essay Prize; by failing to secure election to a prize fellowship at All Souls. After that had come disappointment in an application for a junior post at Bristol, followed by the disaster of the assistant lectureship at Liverpool. The professor there, J.M. Mackay, as Powicke later recalled, 'displayed a well bred, courteous and not unkindly repugnance to my presence', and did not renew him at the end of the probationary year. Tout came to the rescue with an assistant lectureship at Manchester: indeed Tout's encouragement and consistent support were what sustained him through the disappointments and mishaps of this period. Justifiably, he felt undervalued, even slighted. The chair at Queen's gave him at last the established position and security that he had so long sought; that and the favourable reception of his *Loss of Normandy* provided the needed buttress to his confidence. From this point on his career as a scholar went forward from strength to strength.

It is not really surprising that it is easier to see what tenure of the Queen's chair did for Powicke than what Powicke's tenure did for Queen's. It cannot have been an easy place on which to leave a mark, when he came there in 1909. History as a degree subject was in its infancy in the university; it was less respected as an honours course than most other subjects in an arts faculty where student numbers averaged just below two hundred, of whom most were reading for pass degrees. For the ablest in the schools of Northern Ireland in this pre-Troubles period Trinity College Dublin was still a very powerful magnet. Then, five years after Powicke's arrival, there came the outbreak of world war. In 1915 that carried him away to London to work with the War Trade Intelligence Department, and kept him there until after the war had ended. He had not yet fully resumed his duties as professor in 1919 when he was elected to fill the vacancy at Manchester that Tout's retirement had created. Over the war years his teaching had been looked after by Maud Clarke as deputy professor. Clarke, the gifted daughter of the rector of Carnmoney, had been singled out by Powicke for her talent when she came to Queen's in 1910, and he had sent her on to Oxford after she graduated with a brilliant first (as Tout had once despatched Powicke himself in the same circumstances). She made her mark at Oxford as she had at Belfast, and in 1919, at the same time that Powicke quitted the Belfast chair, she was invited back to Oxford to a fellowship and tutorship in medieval history at Somerville College. Maud Clarke's three years as Powicke's very youthful deputy is the flimsy bridge between his tenure and influence and that of his successor at Queen's, James Eadie Todd.

Todd, rather than Powicke, was to be the real founder, as I see it, of the tradition of medieval historical scholarship at Queen's – and of historical scholarship there in the broader sense too, I suspect. He was originally a graduate of Edinburgh, a pupil of the distinguished professor Sir Richard Lodge; like Powicke he had gone on to Oxford and to Balliol, where he too was taught by H.W.C. Davis. Todd was above all a teacher, and published little; his principal interests, as they developed, came to be in the early modern history of England and Ireland, and in modern European history. But when he came to Queen's, his main interest appeared to be in medieval economic history: he had been a collaborator with the great

Professor Paul Vinogradoff in his study of the fourteenth-century honour of Denbigh.[1]

At Queen's, he made a vital contribution to medieval study, first through his own teaching, and secondly by persuading the university, in 1927, to establish an assistant lectureship in medieval history. The first three holders of this new post were all future scholars of distinction: G. R. Potter, later professor at Sheffield and editor of the important text *Gesta Stephani*; H.A. Cronne, Todd's own Queen's pupil and a future professor of medieval history at Birmingham; and R.R. Betts, destined in due time to become the leading British scholar of East European medieval history of his day and Masyryk Professor of Slavonic Studies at the University of London.

When Betts left Queen's in 1934, Todd, keenly alive to the desirability of giving Irish history a high profile in Belfast, shifted the focus of the department's junior post, converting it into an assistant lectureship in Irish history, and resuming himself for the time being the responsibility for all medieval teaching. When Theo Moody, the first assistant lecturer under the new terms, left after four years, Todd made a brilliant second appointment that catered for the interests of both Irish and medieval history, that of D.B. Quinn.

Quinn is, of course, remembered above all as the great historian of Tudor Ireland, but he was also deeply versed in the island's medieval and especially its late medieval history: witness his brilliant chapters in the second volume (covering the years 1169–1534) of the *New History of Ireland* (Oxford, Clarendon Press, 1987), edited by the distinguished Queen's trained medievalist, Art Cosgrove (later President of University College Dublin). Thus Todd, with Quinn, laid foundations for that eminence in Irish medieval study which has been a particular feature of the Queen's history department's distinction ever since.

By good fortune, when Todd retired and Quinn departed at the closing of the Second World War, Todd's chosen successor as professor was Geoffrey Sayles, a scholar who had already developed an interest in Irish medieval history before coming to Belfast. Among Sayles's first appointments to junior posts (raised in number in 1945–6 from one to three) was that of Jack Gray, another medievalist with strong Irish interests. Sayles's distinction and publications – his and H.G. Richardson's *The Irish Parliament in the Middle Ages* appeared in 1952 (London: Geoffrey Cumberledge) – combined with Jack Gray's charisma as a teacher to keep the torch of medieval scholarship burning brightly in the post-war years of Queen's expansion.

Lewis Warren, who came to Queen's in the 1950s as an assistant lecturer just after Sayles's departure, and became Sayles's next-but-one successor in the chair, gave a further injection of enthusiasm and inspiration. Warren grew to be one of the dominant scholars of twelfth- and thirteenth-century British history. His research interest in the Angevin history of Ireland helped to ensure the continued vitality of Irish alongside British and European history in the undergraduate courses and the research programmes of the department that he came to lead; this tradition is being carried forward in the present day on the medieval side through the teaching and distinguished research of Warren's appointee, Dr Marie Therese Flanagan.

The lines of connection that I have been trying to trace in these last few paragraphs lead back, through Lewis Warren, Jack Gray, Geoffrey Sayles and D.B. Quinn, to James Todd rather than to Powicke. It is a notable fact, and one that seems significant to me, that, judged by the very full list of Powicke's publications put together later by his pupils and admirers, there is no sign that his Belfast years stirred in him any serious interest in Irish history, as they did so notably for Todd and Warren, who like him came to Queen's from outside Ireland. But there can be no doubt whatever about the Irish interests of the one brilliant scholar whom Powicke succeeded in bringing forward in his time at Queen's, Maud Clarke.

Although most of Clarke's academic working life was spent in Oxford, she remained always and consciously an Irishwoman; home for her meant County Antrim. I referred to her influence earlier as the flimsy bridge between Powicke's tenure of the Queen's chair and the interest in medieval studies that his successor Todd did so much to foster. There was nothing in the least flimsy, I should stress, about her or her scholarship. She it was who carried the department for Powicke when he was called away to war work, so that the students that Todd inherited were essentially her students – the students of Powicke's prize pupil. Her masterly essays on Edward II's Irish parliaments and on William Windsor's lieutenancy for Edward III in Ireland (in her *Fourteenth Century Studies*, Oxford: Clarendon Press, 1937) attest the ongoing and vivid interest in Irish medieval history of her Oxford years. If cancer had not cut short her career as a scholar there would no doubt have been much more. There can be no doubt either, I think, that it was her work on the Irish parliament and on the Irish version of the *Modus Tenendi Parliamentum* in her *Medieval Representation and Consent* (London: Longmans Green, 1936), that first caught the attention of Sayles's friend Richardson, and so stimulated Sayles's own interest in the subject and in that text in particular, ensuring that when he came to Belfast it was with an already aroused interest in medieval Ireland.

Clarke's undergraduate training, her early teaching experience and her research interests provided the most significant links that I have been able to find between Powicke's days at Queen's and the medievalist circle that he gathered around him at Oxford – in which naturally she figured – and so with Irish medieval scholarship as it has grown at Queen's under Powicke's successors. She also, I should add, provided a link between those academic and historical worlds and the literary world of her friend, fellow scholar and near contemporary at Queen's, Helen Waddell, of whom Norman Vance has written so vividly in this collection (see Chapter 7, 'Helen Waddell and Literary Europe'). Powicke, Maud Clarke, Helen Waddell, Lewis Warren – these really are names to conjure with in the twentieth-century story of British and Irish medieval scholarship. Their achievements and distinctions are eloquent testimony to the way in which an academic institution that is firmly rooted in its own regional community can make a contribution that is significant to the global community of learning.

---

[1] 'Honour' is used in the sense it carries in feudal tenurial law, defined in the *Oxford English Dictionary* as 'a seignory (or lordship) of several manors held under one baron or lord paramount'. Denbigh was one such seignory.

John Bell and
the Quantum World

P.G. BURKE

P.G. BURKE is Emeritus Professor of Mathematical Physics at Queen's University.

John Stewart Bell, the second of John and Annie Bell's four children, was born on 28 July 1928 in the Tates Avenue area of Belfast city. The families of both his parents were Protestant, his father's family coming from Fermanagh and his mother's from Tyrone. Originally his mother's family had come from Scotland, and John Bell's second Christian name was that of her family. At home, Bell was always known as Stewart, only being called John when he went to university.

Bell showed exceptional promise at school, and at home was often known as 'the Prof' because of his very wide reading and knowledge, which he expounded to the family. Indeed at the tender age of eleven he announced to his parents that he intended to be a scientist. It was also at school at about the same age that John Bell first became a vegetarian, which he was to remain for the rest of his life.

After attending the Ulsterville Avenue and Fane Street Elementary schools and the Belfast Technical High School, Bell started his working life in 1944 as a junior laboratory assistant in the physics department at Queen's University. It was here that he came under the beneficent supervision of Professor George Emeleus (then head of department) and Dr Robert Harvey Sloane, who were to guide his early interests in the foundations of quantum theory through discussions and through the loan of books. After a year, Emeleus found some financial support for Bell, and in 1945 he commenced his degree studies, graduating in 1948 with a first-class honours degree in experimental physics. Bell then stayed at Queen's for a further year, obtaining a first-class honours degree in mathematical physics in 1949. He was one of the last students of the famous crystallographer Professor Paul Ewald, a refugee from Germany at Queen's who later became head of the physics department at the Polytechnic Institute of Brooklyn, New York.

In late 1949, Bell was offered a position at the Atomic Energy Research Establishment at Harwell near Oxford, and was assigned by Dr Klaus Fuchs, who was then head of the theoretical physics division, to work on reactor physics. Bell later told Dr Leslie Kerr, who had been a fellow student at Queen's, 'the only odd thing that I noticed was that Fuchs had to go up to London frequently'.[1] Later it became clear that these visits were for questioning, prior to his arrest for espionage in January 1950. After Fuchs's arrest, Bell was assigned to work on accelerator design in the group headed by Bill Walkinshaw. It was while working in Walkinshaw's group that Bell met his future wife, Mary Ross, who had a degree in mathematics and physics from Glasgow University. They started a collaboration on accelerator physics that was to last until the end of Bell's life. They were married in 1954. During the early 1950s at Harwell, John also pursued his long-standing interest in the foundations of quantum theory. This interest was further stimulated by many discussions with Dr Franz Mandl (to which I will return later).

In the autumn of 1953, Bell was granted a year's leave of absence from Harwell to work in the department of mathematical physics at the University of Birmingham, headed by Professor Sir Rudolf Peierls. There he profited from the supervision of Dr Paul Matthews, and in a short while had acquired an up-to-date knowledge of modern theoretical physics. It was during this period at Birmingham that John obtained a proof of the charge conjugation, parity inversion, time reversal (CPTR) theorem, one of the fundamental theorems of elementary particle physics, which formed the first part of his 1956 Birmingham PhD thesis.

Towards the end of the 1950s, the role of Harwell began to change. It had been established to perform basic research on the peaceful uses of atomic energy, but by 1960 the first nuclear power stations had been constructed in the UK and other laboratories had been established to perform research in high energy physics and magnetically confined fusion, which had been undertaken at Harwell. As a result, John and Mary Bell began to think of moving from Harwell. At that time there did not seem to be any university in the UK that could accommodate John's growing interest in elementary particle physics and Mary's interest in accelerator design. The obvious place to go was the European Centre for Nuclear Research (CERN) in Geneva, so in 1960 they resigned their tenured positions at Harwell. John joined the CERN Theory Division and Mary joined the Accelerator Research Group. They were to remain there, apart from rare absences, for the rest of John Bell's life, their positions becoming permanent after a second three-year term.

The Theory Division at CERN has typically 100–120 members, of whom about ten are permanent, the rest being visitors. The permanent members tend to work with the visitors, and Bell was no exception. During the first half of his CERN period his work was closely linked to theoretical problems suggested by the CERN experiments. However, even when confronted with an immediate practical problem, he was always concerned with matters of principle. He was never one to work on a problem without obtaining a full understanding of both the problem and its origins. This led to advances in fields others considered closed. He also found time to pursue his interests in the foundations of quantum theory, which he called his 'hobby'. This was particularly true during his brief leave of absence at the Stanford Linear Accelerator Center (SLAC) in 1963 and later again at CERN.

I will now briefly review the breadth of Bell's research before discussing in more detail his profound contributions to the foundations of quantum theory.

From the time John joined Bill Walkinshaw's group at Harwell until his leave of absence to carry out graduate work at the University of Birmingham in 1953 his research was almost entirely devoted to accelerator physics. The first twenty-one items in his bibliography from 1950 to 1954 were concerned with different aspects of this subject. This included work on the design of the proton synchrotron to be built at CERN, with Sir John Adams, who later became director general of CERN. He also wrote a seminal paper on the algebra of strong focusing, read by all accelerator designers of the day. Mary and John Bell's collaboration on accelerator problems, which had commenced at Harwell, continued at CERN. They wrote several papers on electron cooling, following an idea of Soviet physicists. Also, one of John's most remarkable achievements was the result of combining considerations from accelerator physics with quantum field theory. With Jon Leinaas, who was a research fellow at CERN in the early 1980s, Bell showed that the Unruh effect, which is the field-theoretic relation between acceleration and temperature, is relevant to electron accelerators. This important result brought together Bell's expertise in seemingly very disparate fields. (John Bell's most important papers referred to in this paragraph and in the following paragraphs are reproduced in *Selected Papers of John S. Bell*, edited by M. Bell, K. Gottfried and M. Veltman.)[2]

Turning to Bell's contributions to nuclear and elementary particle physics: I have already mentioned his proof of the CPT theorem while he was still a research student at Birmingham. He also made many other fundamental contributions to nuclear and particle physics while he was at Harwell, covering a very wide range of topics, many with other members of the Theoretical Physics Division. Bell continued to work in elementary particle physics when he arrived at CERN in 1960, writing papers with many visitors to the laboratory in support of the experimental programme. Of particular interest was his influential work on intermediate boson production by neutrinos with Martinus Veltman in 1963, and on the weak interaction of K-mesons with Jack Steinberger in 1965. Veltman and Steinberger were both later to be awarded Nobel Prizes.[3]

Finally, I turn to a discussion of Bell's profound work on the foundations of quantum theory. I have already mentioned that his interest in this subject was kindled by discussions with George Emeleus and with Robert Sloane when he was an undergraduate student at Queen's University. He also had many discussions with Franz Mandl at Harwell and acknowledged these discussions in his 1966 paper published in the *Reviews of Modern Physics*.[4] They discussed von Neumann's work on this subject and, since John could not read German, Franz Mandl translated the relevant sections from von Neumann's famous 1932 book to aid their discussions.[5] As Mandl said later in a personal letter to me, 'I was at the right place at the right time.'

In order to fully appreciate Bell's contributions to the foundations of quantum theory, I will briefly describe the background to his work. During the years immediately following the development of the new quantum theory by Louis de Broglie, Werner Heisenberg and Erwin Schrödinger, in the period from 1924 to 1926, the small population of quantum physicists was intensely occupied not only with the development of the theory and applying it to new areas but also with understanding the conceptual foundations of the theory. The scientists who were most actively involved in this debate were Max Born, Niels Bohr and Albert Einstein, although others joined in the discussions, including de Broglie, Heisenberg, Schrödinger and Wolfgang Pauli.

Einstein himself was, of course, one of the originators of quantum theory, being awarded the Nobel Prize in Physics in 1921 for his famous work, in 1905, on the quantum theory of the photoelectric effect.[6] However, he was deeply sceptical about the probabilistic interpretation of quantum theory put forward by Max Born in 1926. Max Born, in his influential paper on collision theory, had written:

> One does not get an answer to the question, 'What is the state after the collision?' but only to the question, 'How *probable* is a given effect of the collision?'. From the standpoint of quantum theory there is no quantity which causally fixes the effect of a collision in an individual event.

Born's paper had a mixed reception. Several leading physicists found it hard to swallow, including Schrödinger, who is reported to have said to Bohr that he might not have published his papers had he been able to foresee what consequences they would unleash. However, others, including Bohr, Heisenberg and Eugene Wigner, embraced Born's ideas.

Einstein, in particular, took great exception to Born's probabilistic interpretation of quantum theory and in a reply to one of Born's letters, in December 1926, he wrote:

> Quantum mechanics is very impressive. But an inner voice tells me that it is not yet the real thing. The theory produces a good deal but hardly brings us closer to the secrets of the Old One. I am at all events convinced that He does not play dice.

Einstein amplified these views in the great debate on the foundations of quantum theory with Niels Bohr, which commenced in 1926 and went on for many years.

Bell was greatly stimulated by this debate, in which he tended to support Einstein on philosphical issues. He was also struck by the contradiction between von Neumann's apparent proof in his 1932 book that there could be no hidden-variable theory of quantum mechanics and Bohm's presentation of such a theory.

However, probably the greatest stimulus for Bell's work on the foundations of quantum theory came from a paper published by Einstein with two young collaborators, Boris Podolsky and Nathan Rosen in the *Physical Review* in 1935.[7] In this paper, the authors drew attention, by example, to the non-local nature of quantum systems, which run counter to all our instincts. They considered two particles, A and B (say two electrons or two photons), which are initially close together in a given quantum state. The particles then move freely apart in opposite directions. In quantum theory a measurement of, say, the spin component of particle A has an immediate effect on the measurement of the spin component of particle B, however far apart the two particles are. It was this 'spooky action at a distance', as Einstein called it, that he disliked so much.[8]

In their paper Einstein, Podolsky and Rosen introduced the principles of Reality and Locality. The Reality Principle states:

> If, without in any way disturbing a system, we can predict with certainty (i.e. with probability equal to unity) the value of a physical quantity, then there exists an element of physical reality corresponding to that quantity.

The Locality Principle states:

> If two systems have been for a period of time in dynamical isolation from each other, then a measurement on the first system can produce no real change in the other.

Theories satisfying these principles are often called Locally Realistic Theories. In formulating these principles, Einstein, Podolsky and Rosen highlighted a paradox in probabilistic quantum theory.

It is an illustration of Bell's genius that in his most influential paper, 'On the Einstein-Podolsky-Rosen Paradox', he was able to devise a way of experimentally determining whether Quantum Theory or a Locally Realistic Theory is correct.[9] This paper enables experiment to resolve the debate by Einstein, Bohr, Heisenberg, Born and others on the foundations of quantum theory. It changed this subject from a philosophical discussion into an experimental science, which is the only unambiguous way of determining what the 'Old One' intended.

In this paper, Bell introduced quantities which can be constructed from experimental measurements, which satisfy certain inequalities if a locally realistic theory is correct, but which can be violated if quantum theory is correct.

In a beautiful experiment carried out in 1982 by Alain Aspect and his collaborators from the Université Paris-Sud Orsay, it was found that Bell's inequalities were violated, giving convincing confirmation of quantum theory rather than local reality.[10] Had Einstein been alive he could no longer have written:

> ... I still cannot find any fact anywhere which would make it appear likely that that requirement (locality) will have to be abandoned.[11]

The paper by Bell has had an enormous influence on subsequent developments in quantum theory, quantum experiments and quantum technology. In the case of quantum technology, entangled quantum states permit a new way of encoding and processing information with far-reaching implications for quantum computing, quantum communications and quantum cryptography.

The important new observation is that information is not independent of the physical laws used to store and process it. Although modern computers require quantum processes to operate, for example in the operation of computer chips, the information itself is still encoded classically. A new approach is required to treat information as a quantum concept and to ask what new insights can be gained by encoding this information in individual quantum systems; in other words, what happens when both the transmission and the processing of information are governed by quantum laws.

The elementary quantity of classical information is the 'bit', which can take on one of two values, usually 0 or 1. Therefore any physical realisation of a bit needs a system with two well-defined states, e.g. a switch which can be on or off, or a pit in a compact disc which is present or absent. Two-state systems are also used to encode information in quantum systems. However, the novel feature of quantum information is that the quantum bit, or 'qubit' can be in the 0 state and the 1 state at the same time. That is, it is in some coherent combination of these states, with complex coefficients.

This very simple extension has enormous implications, since this linear combination is specified by two continuous numbers representing the relative magnitude and phase of the two states. Hence, in principle, a single qubit contains an infinite amount of information. In practice, a qubit can be represented by the spin of an electron, the polarisation of a photon, two energy levels of an atom, a quantum dot, and in many other ways. A Bell state, which describes the Aspect *et al* experiments, is represented by two qubits.

In 1985, David Deutsch extended the Church-Turing principle, which is the basis of classical computers, to define what is called a universal quantum computer.[12] Over the years, many people have worked on this concept and thousands of papers have been published as well as several books.

In principle, it is known how to build a quantum computer by starting with simple logic gates and connecting them into quantum networks. However, as the number of quantum gates in the network increases serious practical problems arise. Apart from the difficulty of working with single atoms, photons or other quantum systems, the challenge is to prevent the surrounding environment from influencing the interactions that generate the quantum superposition. This process that can spoil the computation is known as decoherence. The task is to engineer sub-microscopic systems in which the qubits affect each other but do not interact with the environment.

In spite of these difficulties, the opportunities which are opened up by quantum computers, quantum communications and quantum cryptography are enormous. For example, quantum algorithms for searching an unsorted list and for factorising large numbers into primes are exponentially more efficient using a quantum computer. In addition, the possibility of carrying out quantum simulations of quantum processes, first suggested by Richard Feynman in 1982, is an area which is currently exciting many scientists.[13] For example, at the moment classical computers run out of steam in the full simulation of two-electron atoms in intense laser fields, hence the possible future use of quantum computing to solve problems in this area is of considerable interest to researchers in the department of applied mathematics and theoretical physics at Queen's.

Finally, considerable progress has been made in recent years in the teleportation of quantum states and in quantum cryptography. Both of these require for their implementation the combination of classical and quantum communication channels and both have been experimentally realised.

Hence in the present situation where classical computing and communications may soon reach fundamental limits, the quantum advances stimulated by Bell's work have the potential for truly revolutionary innovation. The realisation of this enormous potential provides a grand challenge for twenty-first century scientists and engineers.

In conclusion, John Bell was greatly respected by all who knew him. He was modest and unassuming, and had a delightful sense of humour. He had a lifelong collaboration with his wife, Mary, which he acknowledged in the preface to his book on quantum philosophy.[14]

Bell was elected a fellow of the Royal Society in 1972, and in the last eight years of his life he received many awards as the full significance of his exceptional achievements became fully realised. These included honorary degrees from both Queen's University Belfast and Trinity College Dublin in 1988. He was nominated for a Nobel Prize and, if he had not died suddenly and tragically from a stroke on 1 October 1990, he undoubtedly would have been awarded it.

---

[1] A quotation from my personal correspondence with Dr Leslie Kerr.
[2] M. Bell, K. Gottfried and M. Veltman, *Quantum Mechanics, High Energy Physics and Accelerators: Selected Papers of John S. Bell (with commentary)* (Singapore, New Jersey, London, Hong Kong: World Scientific Publishing Company, 1995).
[3] Ibid.
[4] J.S. Bell, 'On the Problem of Hidden Variables in Quantum Theory', *Reviews of Modern Physics* 38 (1966): 447–52.
[5] J. von Neumann, *Mathematical Foundations of Quantum Mechanics*, tr. Robert T. Beyer (Princeton: University Press, 1955).
[6] A. Einstein, *Annalen der Physik* vol. 17 (1905), 132.
[7] A. Einstein, B. Podolsky and N. Rosen, 'Can Quantum-mechanical Description of Physical Reality be Considered Complete?', *Physical Review* 47 (1935): 777–80.
[8] This quotation is referred to in many articles about Einstein. It most likely originated in conversation between Einstein and other scientists.
[9] J.S. Bell, 'On the Einstein-Podolsky-Rosen Paradox', *Physics* 1 (1964): 195–200.
[10] A. Aspect, P. Grangier and G. Roger, 'Experimental Realization of Einstein-Podolsky-Rosen-Bohm Gedanken Experiment: A New Violation of Bell's Inequalities', *Physical Review Letters* 49 (1982): 91–4; A. Aspect, J. Dalibard

and G. Roger, 'Experimental Test of Bell's Inequalities Using Time-varying Analyzers', *Physical Review Letters* 49 (1982): 1804–7.

[11] This quotation of Einstein's is made in many discussions of Bell's work without reference to the original source.

[12] D. Deutsch, *Quantum Theory, the Church-Turing Principle and the Universal Quantum Computer*, (London: Proceedings of the Royal Society, 1985), 73–90.

[13] A.J.G. Hey and R.W. Allen (eds.) *Feynman Lectures on Computation* (Reading, Massachusetts: Perseus Books, 1996).

[14] J.S. Bell, *Speakable and Unspeakable in Quantum Mechanics: Collected Papers on Quantum Philosophy* (Cambridge: Cambridge University Press, 1987).

Philip Larkin and Belfast Literary Culture

EDNA LONGLEY

EDNA LONGLEY is Professor Emerita in the School of English, Queen's University.

At a book launch in the Bookshop at Queen's an English novelist remarked: 'Surely that's not Philip Larkin up there!' He was puzzled by Larkin's presence on the bookshop's frieze among such Irish literary worthies as J.M. Synge and Medbh McGuckian. Equally, one could ask what Larkin (1922–1985) has to do with Belfast literary culture beyond the fact that he was sub-librarian at Queen's from 1950 to 1955, in a misty Belfast which knew nothing of book launches, and wrote some poems here? Indeed, 'Philip Larkin and Belfast Literary Culture' is a title I was given for the 'Queen's Thinkers' conference rather than one I chose. Yet the problems raised by 'Philip Larkin and Belfast Literary Culture' may be more intriguing than an obvious topic like 'John Hewitt and Belfast Literary Culture'.

To start with, three problems. First, Larkin didn't think of himself as a 'thinker' let alone a Queen's one. He moaned in November 1951, 'This time next week ... I'm featured in a *Brains Trust* at the English Society. Holy God! ... I suppose I'm there to provide comic relief'.[1] More seriously, when interviewed by Anthony Thwaite about his *Oxford Book of Twentieth Century English Verse* (Oxford: Clarendon Press, 1973), Larkin thus excused his failure to write a preface: 'I'm not a theorist, I'm not a critic, I'm not an academic.'[2] And in a later interview: 'I've never had "ideas" about poetry.'[3] In fact, Larkin saw the rise of university criticism as corrupting literature. Writing to Thwaite in 1974 he satirised the poet-academic Donald Davie to the tune of 'Daisy, Daisy':

>Davie, Davie,
>Give me a bad review;
>That's your gravy,
>Telling chaps what to do.
>Forget about sense and passion
>As long as it's in the fashion –
>But let's be fair,
>It's got you a chair,
>And a billet in Frogland too.[4]

Davie was then a professor at Stanford University, California, and had a house in France.

Second, aside from his closeness to Kingsley Amis, Larkin was a literary loner. He was neither coterie material nor one of those messianic poets like W.B. Yeats who need cohorts, disciples, a creative community, a cultural revival, a national revolution, global apocalypse. He might have contributed to the local BBC radio programme *The Arts in Ulster*, or reviewed for the Queen's magazine *Q*, but he insisted on solitude as the essential condition of the lyric poet, the essential condition for writing lyric poetry. A poem from 1951, 'Best Society', shows the poet retreating to his upstairs rooms in the now-vanished 30 Elmwood Avenue. The poem dramatises a recurrent position in Larkin's poetry: the artist's necessary refusal of the social world:

> Viciously, then, I lock my door.
> The gas-fire breathes. The wind outside
> Ushers in evening rain. Once more
> Uncontradicting solitude
> Supports me on its giant palm;
> And like a sea-anemone
> Or simple snail, there cautiously
> Unfolds, emerges, what I am.[5]

This is a portrait of Larkin doing his kind of thinking. Later, his Belfast retrospects would nostalgically evoke the cloistered space of evenings devoted to the Muse.

Third, 'Belfast Literary Culture' not only implies writers hanging out, but a kind of localism or regionalism that Larkin never embraced. He and Amis are often attached by critics, if problematically again, to the 1950s non-metropolitan formation dubbed simply 'the Movement'. But these writers' horizon was provincial (an English provincialism) rather than regional. They assumed a provincial–metropolitan rather than regional–cosmopolitan literary axis. To quote from Blake Morrison's *The Movement*: 'This provincialism is not to be confused with "regionalism", a mode of writing which the Movement saw as consisting of sentimental, and usually Celtic, celebration of one's "roots".'[6] Hewitt's Ulster regionalism is a case in point: his belief that a writer must be 'a rooted man'. Larkin and Hewitt coincided in Belfast but they made no literary common cause. When Amis won the 1955 Somerset Maugham award (which required the recipient to travel), Larkin noted that a travel book by Amis was about as likely as 'a space-thriller by John Hewitt'.[7] A regionalist manifesto by Philip Larkin would have been unlikely too. For Larkin and Amis, the literary cult of 'Abroad' and the literary cult of 'roots' were equally objectionable. In 1967, after a decade in Hull, Larkin joked: 'I am not even turning into a regional poet, with his clay pipe and acknowledged corner in the snug of the Cat and Fuddle.'[8]

He introduced Douglas Dunn's anthology *A Rumoured City: New Poets from Hull* (Newcastle upon Tyne: Bloodaxe Books, 1982) by saying just that Hull is 'as good a place to write as any'. Larkin's Hull, like his Belfast, primarily constitutes a neutral cloister for the Muse's visitations, for 'uncontradicting solitude'. He goes on to call Hull 'a city that is in the world, yet sufficiently on the edge of it to have a different resonance. Behind Hull is the plain of Holderness, lonelier and lonelier ...'[9]

Now to reverse everything said so far. Larkin is, after all, a poet of subtle masks and dialectics, not to mention jokes, ironies and teases. His refusals affirm principles. First, Larkin is a hugely important thinker *about* poetry as well as in it. Second, Belfast influenced his poetry. Third, he influenced the poets who, in the 1960s, would be viewed collectively as 'Belfast poets'. Overall, Larkin's time in Belfast can be seen as a key moment in the complex interactions that continue to shape modern poetry in these islands.

On my first point: Larkin's contribution to the aesthetics of modern poetry is both considerable and underrated. Even if he wrote no systematic *ars poetica*, he left a significant body of criticism – reviews, interviews, and the writings about jazz which are disguised poetry criticism. And when Larkin disavows theory, he is really questioning other poets' theories. Here his main butt is the 'modernism' of T.S. Eliot and Ezra Pound, or more strictly its academic exegesis. In 1964 Larkin complained to Ian Hamilton that 'poetry seems to have got into the hands of a critical industry which is concerned with culture in the abstract, and this I ... lay at the door of Eliot and Pound'.[10] By 'culture in the abstract' – as opposed to culture freshly lived – Larkin means the literariness of modernism: all those quotations in Eliot's *Waste Land* and Pound's *Cantos*. In a broadcast of 1958 he called poetry 'a skill easily damaged by self-consciousness'.[11] Since self-consciousness infects content as much as style, he also doubted a poet's duty to be topical. In 1957, contributing to a *London Magazine* symposium on 'The Writer in His Age', he said: 'A man may believe that what we want at present is a swingeing good novel on the state of this or the fate of that, but his imagination remains unstirred except by notions of renunciation or the smell of a certain brand of soap.'[12] Thus Larkin challenged an increase in poetic self-consciousness for which he mainly blamed the academy. And he distrusted critical and political fashions that 'tell poets what to do', to apply his Davie lampoon. All this indicates that Larkin's own 'idea' of poetry is extremely pure. It combines an aroma of *fin de siècle* aestheticism with a central tenet of romanticism: the primacy of inspiration. Poetry depends on what 'stirs' the imagination. In 1957 again, he insisted: 'writing a poem is ... not an act of the will ... Whatever makes a poem successful is not an act of the will.'[13] The distinctiveness of Larkin's imaginative world derives from its truth to his stirrings and feelings – however dark some of these may be.

Biographical revelations about Larkin have at least corrected the false impression that he is a social-realist poet rather than a Romantic aesthete who explores disturbing psychic zones. Similarly, his formal achievement is now properly recognised. Larkin was more steeped in literature, more profoundly allusive, than he pretended. His hostility to the Eliot–Pound hegemony (although his poetic taste was much more eclectic than some suppose) signifies commitment to what Yeats calls 'those traditional metres that have developed with the language'.[14] In one interview Larkin sums up 'writing poetry' in Yeatsian terms as 'playing off the natural rhythms and word order of speech against the artificialities of rhyme and metre', and describes what he learned from Yeats and W.H. Auden as 'the management of lines, the formal distancing of emotion'.[15] Larkin completed all his creative apprenticeships during his Belfast years. He wrote three-quarters of *The Less Deceived* (Hessle, East Yorkshire: The Marvell Press, 1955) in the city, and the first poem in the collection, 'Lines on a Young Lady's Photograph Album', at once *ars poetica* and love poem, consummates what has happened to his inner landscape: 'What grace / Your candour thus confers upon her face! / How overwhelmingly persuades / That this is a real girl in a real place // In every sense empirically true'.[16] This apostrophe to photography defines Larkin's aesthetic as an empirical openness to sensation that engenders new kinds of reality. At the same time, his 'real' and 'true' are not limited to the material plane or to the album's implicitly Northern Irish scenes: they aspire to the condition of symbol.

At another level (to move on to my second point) the poem proves that Larkin got out more in Belfast than his self-images imply. Later in the evening he would leave the cloister, drink, play bridge, listen to jazz. The smaller, more collegiate, less managerial Queen's of that day gave him a busy social life and two intense amours. The 'real girl in a real place' was Winifred Arnott, a graduate of the English department, then working in the Library. And, insofar as she is the Muse of *The Less Deceived*, perhaps her real place obliquely lights the poems, as does the real girl's symbolic translation. Larkin finally says of the Hull anthology: 'These poems are not about Hull, yet it is unseen in all of them, the permission of a town that lets you write.'[17]

A hint of how Belfast affected Larkin's aesthetic lies in his phrase 'the formal distancing of emotion'. As well as form, Belfast gave his poetry distance or perspective. Larkin's sexual liaisons and their poetic fallout were eased by distance from his family and relationships in England. A poem about 'Arrival' in Belfast hails a newness (whose 'ignorance of me / Seems a kind of innocence') that buries the past. He christens the city, improbably, a 'milk-aired Eden'.[18] As with Larkin's personal past, so with his English cultural affiliations. Just after returning to England he wrote 'The Importance of Elsewhere' (1955), a poem about the enabling effects of distance and difference, the disabling effects of closeness:

> Lonely in Ireland, since it was not home,
> Strangeness made sense. The salt rebuff of speech,
> Insisting so on difference, made me welcome:
> Once that was recognised, we were in touch ...[19]

Here Belfast's exoticism, its different language – not just voice – is recalled as liberating. Later, the poem says of England: 'These are my customs and establishments / It would be much more serious to refuse. / Here no elsewhere underwrites my existence.'[20] This is another *ars poetica*. In Ireland Larkin felt less spiritually (not politically) coerced by English 'customs and establishments'. He felt freer to explore both his own 'strangeness' and an England which Ireland's strangeness brought into focus. 'Church-Going', often seen as a quintessentially 'English' poem, was sparked off in 1954 by a Northern Irish church.[21] Yet, despite the ineradicable reflex whereby he 'thrilled to the accent of that sharp skylined city',[22] Larkin was wary of either going native in Belfast or becoming a professional expat. His memoir of 'The Library I Came to' in *Gown Literary Supplement* (1984) concludes: 'I was sorry to go, but I had been at Queen's nearly five years, and I could not see myself as an Anglo-Ulsterman with a cottage at Cushendall and an adopted accent.'[23]

Finally, 'The Importance of Elsewhere', the importance of difference, distance and strangeness, applies to poetic tradition as well as poetic imagination. Larkin had in a sense already visited Ireland by so thoroughly internalising Yeats. The story of modern poetry in these islands pivots on criss-crossings between Irish, British and American points of the aesthetic compass. Thus Larkin began writing poetry at the intersection of several long-term and short-term literary histories. These included the Irish Revival, modernism and the poetry of the 1930s (Auden and Louis MacNeice). Further, as regards Belfast literary culture, where these histories were also about to be reactivated, Larkin arrived – and left – between the ebbing of Hewitt's regionalism and the advent of new poets, in particular Seamus Heaney, Derek Mahon and Michael Longley.

What links Larkin with these poets? The Belfast Group run by Philip Hobsbaum in the early 1960s was certainly not the only begetter of a new 'Northern Irish' poetry. But two conduits between Larkin and the Group should be mentioned. First, Larkin's closest literary friend in Belfast, the great polylingual, polymathic Arthur Terry, who sadly died in February 2004, was a Group member – 'an indispensable presence', to quote one obituarist. Second, Hobsbaum took many of his own bearings from Larkin. But Hobsbaum read Larkin in fairly simple social-realist terms. For more profound assimilation we must look to Larkin's presence in the first collections of the three poets named above. First, as I have said, Larkin's example encouraged poets to be true to their own stirrings rather than to fixed ideas about poetry's subject matter or about where it might be written. In that sense, regional and provincial horizons merge and metropolises become irrelevant. Second, Larkin's influence is most deeply embedded at a formal level, and the formal level is where influence most deeply counts. All three poets are noted for their reworking of traditional forms. And while other precursors also mattered, Larkin was their most immediate model for how traditional forms might negotiate the world of 1960. Following on from MacNeice and Auden, he brought Yeats up to date. Perhaps he realised his impact. Larkin chaired the committee which gave the three poets I have named Eric Gregory awards (a UK award for poets under thirty) in the mid 1960s. Writing to Arthur Terry, he said that he liked seeing 'those fresh young Irish faces'.[24] Fresh, alas, no longer.

Of course, the world of 1960 was to change utterly in Belfast. And when some critics later chided Northern Ireland's poets for not tackling the Troubles in more direct or *engagé* ways, Larkin's aesthetic example, reductively termed 'the well-made poem', would sometimes be blamed for depoliticising them in advance (Larkin as *perfide* Albion's secret weapon). That is, most poets went on responding to what stirred their imaginations rather than to critical or political pundits 'telling chaps what to do'. They did not give up on poetic complexity, on 'the formal distancing of emotion'. One of Philip Larkin's legacies to Belfast literary culture, then, is that we have fewer bad Troubles poems than might otherwise be the case.

---

[1] Philip Larkin, *Selected Letters of Philip Larkin 1940–1985*, ed. Anthony Thwaite (London: Faber & Faber, 1992), 177.
[2] Philip Larkin, *Further Requirements: Interviews, Broadcasts, Statements and Book Reviews*, ed. Anthony Thwaite (London: Faber & Faber, 2001), 102.
[3] Philip Larkin, *Required Writing: Miscellaneous Pieces 1955–1982* (London: Faber & Faber, 1983), 76.
[4] Larkin, *Selected Letters*, 501–2.

5. Philip Larkin, *Collected Poems*, ed. Anthony Thwaite (London: Faber & Faber, 1988), 56.
6. Blake Morrison, *The Movement* (Oxford: Oxford University Press, 1980; London: Methuen, 1986), 61.
7. Larkin, *Selected Letters*, 244.
8. Ibid., 393.
9. Larkin, *Further Requirements*, 128.
10. Ibid., 19.
11. Ibid., 78.
12. Ibid., 4.
13. Larkin, *Required Writing*, 84.
14. W.B. Yeats, 'A General Introduction for My Work', *Essays and Introductions* (London: Macmillan, 1961), 522.
15. Larkin, *Required Writing*, 71, 67.
16. Larkin, *Collected Poems*, 71.
17. Larkin, *Further Requirements*, 128.
18. Larkin, *Collected Poems*, 51.
19. Ibid., 104.
20. Ibid., 104.
21. Ibid., 97.
22. Larkin, *Selected Letters*, 393.
23. *Gown Literary Supplement* (1984); reprinted in *Further Requirements*.
24. Arthur Terry told Michael Longley about the contents of this letter.

Masterclass in University Leadership

Eric Ashby's Vice-chancellorship of Queen's, 1950–1959

PETER FROGGATT

SIR PETER FROGGATT is a former Vice-chancellor and President of Queen's University and Past President of the British Medical Association.

PROLOGUE

Early in 1949 Professor Eric Ashby (1904–1992), Harrison professor of botany and director of the botanical laboratories at the University of Manchester, was approached by Queen's to succeed Sir David Lindsay Keir as vice-chancellor. He demurred, then declined: he was building his department into one of the finest in the country while pursuing his own seminal researches and extending his national activities, all of which were combining to '… rank him as one of the outstanding professors of botany in the twentieth century'.[1] He had already turned down invitations to abandon lecture room and laboratory – notably to be vice-chancellor of the Australian National University (which he had helped to plan) and of the University of Sydney (where he had held the chair of botany) and Australian Minister in Moscow (where he had been scientific counsellor and chargé d'affaires at the Australian Legation, 1945–46).[2] Re-approached by Queen's in the summer of 1949 he swithered, then accepted, much to the surprise (and disappointment) of the scientific fraternity. He had no delusions about the consequences – put starkly, they spelled the end of his experimental career – but the wider challenges triumphed: as he later confided 'I decided … that I was more interested in people than in ideas; in teaching and educational issues than in pure science; and in solving problems about people rather than problems about plants.'[3] It was a pivotal decision for him and a providential one for Queen's.

ASHBY'S BACKGROUND

When Ashby, with his wife, Helen, and their two teenage sons, Michael and Peter, stepped off the boat that autumn morning in 1950, he knew little of Queen's beyond its vital statistics and potted history. He had no first-hand knowledge of its 'special relationship' with the local community, nor of the problems arising from the structure of that society and of Ireland's troubled history which the Queen's Colleges and then the Queen's University of Belfast had very largely been created to address. Ashby was, in fact, a deeply rooted Englishman, though a much-travelled one, as well as a scholar of high intelligence and wide culture.

He was born on 24 August 1904 in north Leyton, east London, the eldest of the three sons of Herbert Charles Ashby, a commercial clerk and later accountant of Bromley, Kent, and Helena Maria Ashby (neé Chater), daughter of a merchant navy captain who had a naturalist's interests and an extensive library in which Ashby would often browse.[4] He entered the City of London School in 1916, a bright student excelling in sciences and a good enough violinist to win a gold medal at the London Academy of Music. In 1923 he entered the Royal College of Science and Technology (later to be Imperial College of Science and Technology, University of London) with the Mortimer Scholarship and graduated ARCS, DIC and BSc with first-class honours in botany and geology and the Forbes Medal. He spent that summer in Germany learning the language well enough to translate Henrik Lundergårdh's *Klima und Boden in Ihrer Wirkung Auf das Pflanzenleben*, published as *Environment and Plant Development*, and he later co-authored, with his wife, *German–English Botanical Terminology* (London: Thomas Murby and Company, 1938).[5] He returned to Imperial, spent two years (1929–31) in the USA on a Commonwealth Fund Fellowship, mainly in Chicago, and returned to a lectureship at Imperial in 1931 and marriage (on 26 December) to Elizabeth Helen Margaret Farries, a plant physiologist, daughter of a farmer from Risk, Castle Douglas, in Scotland.

In 1935 Ashby became reader in botany at the University of Bristol, declined a chair at the University of Manitoba in 1936, but accepted one at the University of Sydney and set sail in late 1937.[6] Ashby's talents as organiser, administrator and communicator as well as teacher and scientist now flourished; and his value as an interpreter and facilitator to the public of scientific concepts and government policies emerged and was invaluable during the war. He served on many university and government committees, soon becoming chairman of most – a portent of the future. Many tempting opportunities in administration and policy-making posts awaited him on his return to Sydney from Moscow in 1946 where he had been scientific counsellor and chargé d'affaires at the Australian Legation, but he preferred to continue his academic life, and from Sydney accepted the Harrison Chair in Manchester (1947) from where, as related, he came as vice-chancellor to Queen's in 1950, at a pivotal point in the development of his career and Queen's fortunes.

ASHBY AT QUEEN'S

CHARACTER AND PERSONALITY

Ashby made an immediate and favourable impact even on the more xenophobic-leaning members of the university; his initial welcome from a senior member of the academic staff, who allegedly referred to him as 'the fifth wheel on the wagon', and other such gratuitous expressions of faint praise from colleagues were short-lived minority views. He was tall (6' 3"); balding in a way which enhanced his height of brow and courtliness of manner; of patrician, if somewhat austere, appearance behind his uncompromising steel-rimmed spectacles; and he radiated dignity without pomposity – a difficult feat. In repose there was a certain hauteur, though not the arrogance which the artist, Ruskin Spear, captured in the portrait of Ashby at Queen's. With his instinctive formality and aura of intellectual power, he could appear intimidating, but his smile, given freely in private and at social gatherings, was winning, while the twinkling eyes disclosed the warmth and humour beneath.

Ashby was an outstanding speaker and, unusually, one for all seasons and for all occasions; but his seeming self-assurance, his style, clarity and impeccable taste, which enthralled many and varied audiences, were not instinctive but the result of meticulous preparation and critical rehearsal – the garden before breakfast and the bathroom in front of the shaving mirror being his preferred stages.[7] He shrank from extempore speeches, which he hated ('Not worth the paper they're written on, Peter') but when unavoidable the result was invariably, and to his intense annoyance, below his customary high standard. He was a consummate chairman, a skill hard won and based on carefully acquired procedural expertise and preliminary preparation, often far into the night. When, as chancellor, he stayed with me at the vice-chancellor's residence, Lennoxvale Lodge, he would say at bedtime, 'I think I'll retire now, and let Peter get on with reading his [working] papers'; this was more a faithful reflection of his own industry than any generous judgement on mine! When I became vice-chancellor of Queen's in 1976 he gave me his well-thumbed and annotated copy of Sir Reginald Palgrave's *The Chairman's Handbook*,[8] inscribed to me with the wise words '[to use] ... only to intimidate persons who try to move amendments to amendments'.

Ashby's wider interests were intellectual and cultural, mainly musical. A talented violinist since schooldays, he played both violin and viola in amateur groups and practised assiduously in the Lodge in Lennoxvale, a routine which he later was to follow in the Master's Lodge at Clare College, Cambridge, in the garden cabin at his cottage in Brandon, Suffolk, and in the enlarged sitting room of 22 Eltisley Avenue in Cambridge, which he often shared with his engineering son and fellow FRS, Michael. Constitutionally robust, a non-smoker of spare build and temperate habits, he had a lifelong disinterest in all ball games and organised sports (he said that carrying the domestic coals around the capacious, three-storey Lennoxvale Lodge and walking around the campus was exercise enough). However, he always enjoyed a bathe and regularly, in season, swam before breakfast in the unappealing lake at Lennoxvale; a home-made diving-board long survived, a silent witness to his sole physical pastime and a cherished relic.

Material comforts, worldly goods and the 'good life' interested him little and his estate was probated at a modest £151,122. When we add to these attributes his high scientific and personal rectitude, which he valued above all else,[9] and his stern sense of duty, then, despite lack of any 'Ulster connection', Ashby, when he arrived at Queen's, was supremely equipped to face whatever challenges lay ahead.

HIGHER EDUCATIONAL STRATEGY

Ashby's 'idea of a university', to borrow the title of John Henry (later Cardinal) Newman's 1859 seminal book,[10] was essentially an amalgam of Newman's 'Liberal Education whereby the intellect is disciplined for its own sake' and of vocational education where acquiring readily usable and useful skills is paramount. Ashby frequently stated this credo, seldom more clearly than in his vice-chancellor's report for 1956–7:

> Universities ... offer opportunities both to the student who wishes to acquire self-fulfilment without reference to any professional training and to the student who wishes to acquire professional skills and nothing more. *This is as it should be. The country needs both kinds of people* ... [italics mine][11]

This idea had a lengthy pedigree and for long had been widely debated, including by Ashby himself. (The 'liberal' culture was often labelled 'value-free' and the 'vocational' one 'value-driven', the 'value' in question presumably being associated with immediate, 'useful', tangible return.) Given its unique position in Northern Ireland, Queen's in reality had no choice but to accept this idea, or rather to continue to accept it, since the Queen's Colleges and even Newman's Catholic University and their various forebears and collaterals had accepted it also. Ashby saw his role clearly: it was to ensure an equitable balance of treatment, respect, resources and standards between the two cultures. He also believed that mere co-existence would be inadequate; symbiosis and synergies were needed to add value to both.

It is tempting to see in his thinking a biological analogy, a form of cross-fertilisation which could weld the advantages of hybrid vigour and robustness ('heterosis') onto the beauty but vulnerability of the pure strains to make the finished products more adaptable to the shifting challenges of the time. No doubt this is fanciful; but heterosis was an enduring research interest of Ashby's who was, naturally enough, comfortable with biological concepts and often in his reasoning appealed to them. When he and I discussed Queen's policy options after the publication of the Chilver Report on 23 March 1982[12] and the simultaneous publication of the government's dismissive *Statement*,[13] which immediately trumped Chilver's main recommendations, Ashby said to me: 'Consider that the government-proposed new institution [University of Ulster] is a novel and threatening mutant or some such (which we will say it is or could be) which suddenly springs up in an existing ecosystem, how best (in retrospect) should the existing members have reacted?', and he boxed the historical biological compass from dinosaurs to the Spanish flu.

Ashby recognised that the constitution of Queen's, based on the liberal ethos of the pre-First World War British legislative establishment and associated mainly with R.B. Haldane,[14] was adequate to meet his objectives; no restructuring involving the Queen's statutes would be necessary. As the 'value-free' lobby feared, he wished to expand the provision of 'value-driven' science and technology, though not at the former's expense. He also planned to improve the quality of the academic staff, raise Queen's national profile while fostering 'town and gown', increase the so-called 'unit of resource' (roughly, a measure of the resources available per student), modernise and expand the university's stock and provisions for staff and student alike, and streamline the administration; an ambitious programme which he largely completed. He was not concerned to increase student numbers if at the expense of standards: he anticipated only modest growth and was surprised at the 17 per cent achieved during his tenure. Nor would he consider intervening to distort the market forces determining ethnic, gender or geographic mix in the student intake, and these in fact hardly changed during the nine years of his vice-chancellorship. Rather than list the formidable enabling decisions made towards these goals I will, more helpfully, focus on Ashby's management style and how he kept up the momentum.

MANAGEMENT STYLE

Ashby was a (benevolent) authoritarian in the guise of a participatory democrat, working within a democratic framework largely controlled by ever-watchful academics and within a labyrinthine structure for decision-taking resulting from a university's then constitutional diffusion of power. Getting his way would be difficult but he knew how to do it; as he wrote, '[In a university] the art of using authority is to secure consent: the good administrator is not a boss but a persuader.'[15] Having early won the confidence of the staff he set out to 'plant', with key members and in impeccably informal settings such as over tea, in the bus or train or at other seemingly chance meetings, ideas which he favoured, and would feign surprise when these surfaced later, as someone else's ideas, for determination by committees which he chaired and without him having formally proposed or publicly supported them anywhere. If this manoeuvre failed he had others, though always within (if sometimes just about within) the rubric of 'persuasion'. He rarely gave orders other than to functionaries; he didn't have to. Always he appeared as the model 'participatory democrat'.

THE PROFESSORIATE

Ashby's top priority was to improve the quality of the professoriate; the hidden agenda was to discourage parochialism in thought and action. The board of curators readily ceded to him the necessary wide discretionary powers to seek out younger scholars or scientists and invite the likeliest to interview. As he recalled:

> [I would] visit three leaders in the field ... and ask each to give me three names of potential candidates who are not yet distinguished but who would be likely to do distinguished work ... in the next ten years ... In this way we attracted to Queen's ... a number of young men who were astonished to have been invited. I would say to them "if you haven't been invited to leave Queen's for another chair in five years (though I hope you'd not accept the invitation), we will think we made a mistake".[16]

This procedure, later to become impossible and even illegal, proved successful: his first five appointments to science-based chairs became fellows of the Royal Society and many in other disciplines became equally prominent, while many lecturers progressed to chairs at Queen's and elsewhere.

FINANCE

Equally pressing was finance. For historical reasons Queen's was less well funded than its British counterparts. Furthermore, the University Grants Committee's (UGC) writ did not run in Northern Ireland; it could only advise the Northern Ireland government on funding to Queen's if invited to do so and its advice was not binding. The UGC had in fact been invited to visit (and accepted) in 1948, two years before Ashby joined Queen's, and visited again in 1952 and 1958. The improved outcome, however, did not satisfy Ashby who decided to exercise his freedom to seek extra funds from the Ministry of Education (NI) directly. He told me that he did so only once, for (extra) recurrent funds; he told the Stormont minister how much he needed, and got it. (He also asked for extra support for his extremely ambitious capital programme, and got that too.) As a result of his persuasiveness and personal standing with the UGC and Stormont and their goodwill to Queen's, during his tenure the total income of the university more than doubled in money terms (80 per cent in real terms) but the portion from government grants nearly tripled; with the accompanying low growth in student numbers this meant a handsome increase in the 'unit of resource'. All staff benefited, including junior academic staff, long neglected due to a strongly prevalent residual belief (held also by Ashby) in the creative spur of attic, midnight oil and handwritten papers. Ashby's eloquence could not, however, win for Queen's parity of funding with its British counterparts; this bastion only finally yielded in the early 1970s to Sir Arthur Vick's (vice-chancellor, 1966–76) compelling statistics and the prorogation of Stormont in March 1972.

STUDENTS

Students were high on Ashby's agenda. The 1950s were years of a campus tranquillity later hardly credible and in a society more at ease with itself than at any time before or since: such causes célèbres as Suez, Hungary and apartheid passed with scant disruption. The collegiate spirit and respect for, even deference to, seniority and authority were alive and well, and the Student Representative Council was content with its single long-established seat on Senate for its President (if a graduate), and even more content to rely on Ashby to promote its modest agenda. Ashby didn't fail them.

The new Students' Union building was a favourite Ashby project. After initial doubts, and the inadequacy of likely funding for a conversion and development of Lanyon's Deaf and Blind Institution on the Lisburn Road, he laid the seeds of ultimately successful plans to place the Students' Union in a then unavailable campus-centre site (the then Queen's Elms). He also laid final plans for the future

Malone Road residences; facilitated the growth of the student health service; paved the way for a full-time career and appointments service; welcomed the appearance of the student magazine *Gown* (in April 1955); planned the reconfiguration of the library and the Queen's Chambers extension; and organised lectures by notables including periodic ones on a Wednesday afternoon (a 'free-from-teaching' time) in the Whitla Hall, which was often filled (1,500 of a student body of some 3,500): I remember 'standing-room only' for the historian A.J.P. Taylor and the establishment savant Noel Annan. Ashby even warned students against wasting their time on endless committees running their own affairs. His classic *The Rise of the Student Estate* evidences his enduring interest.[17]

EXTERNAL PROFILE

Ashby's growing international standing inevitably helped to raise the university's profile. His extramural activities during his time at Queen's were mind-boggling. Added to endless local speaking and social engagements and committees to do with adult education, he was chairman of the organising committee for the visit to Belfast in 1952 of the British Association for the Advancement of Science, chairman of the Northern Ireland Advisory Council for Education (1953–8) and vice-president of the Council for Encouragement of Music and the Arts (CEMA) (1954–8).

In Britain he was a member of the government's Tizard Advisory Council on Scientific Policy (1950–3), of the Advisory Council on Scientific and Industrial Research (1954–60), chairman of the Scientific Grants Committee of the Department of Scientific and Industrial Research (1955–6) and of its Postgraduate Grants Committee (1956–60), vice-chairman of the Association of Universities of the British Commonwealth (1959–61), a member of the Nuffield Provincial Hospitals Trust (1951–9) and of the University Grants Committee (1959–61), and of various sub-committees and working parties of these, and an active member of the UK Committee of Vice-Chancellors and Principals (1950–9), though he repeatedly declined to hold office.

Abroad, he was in a group commissioned by the Inter-University Council (IUC) to report on higher education in East Africa (1954) including a sub-group which visited British East African territories, and he was adviser to the IUC on universities in Nigeria and Ghana (1955) and chairman of a Carnegie Corporation-sponsored commission to advise on all post-secondary education in Nigeria (1959–61).[18] In all he was to visit West Africa some ten times on assignments. The large iceberg hidden below this impressive tip included guest lectures, ad hoc consultations with many colleagues eager for his advice, one book and many shorter publications.[19]

More parochially, he fostered connections with the 'town' which had been previously assumed or ignored. Belfast's great commercial days were history but the new post-war and post-heavy industry society evolving required the university to engage more actively with it, and Ashby assumed the crucial role of interlocutor and interpreter for the respective cultures of 'gown' and 'town' too readily in Northern Ireland stereotyped as respectively unworldly bumblers and avaricious philistines inhabiting completely different worlds.[20] Ashby was knighted (KB) in 1956 and appointed to the Order of St John in 1958.

THE ADMINISTRATION

Ashby also gave close thought to the administration vital to facilitate his plans. Later he was to write much good sense about it. Oddly, perhaps, he did little except to improve facilities virtually unchanged since the university's foundation. In truth he saw no need to; the existing structures were adequate for his unchanging maxim: 'In the eyes of professors all administrators are an evil [so I] say to myself every morning "I am an evil" but am I a necessary evil?', with the answer an emphatic 'yes'. He believed that lay administrators should confine themselves to translating into action policies decided elsewhere, mainly by academics, though he understood the need for professionally qualified ones such as accountants. He was ever alive to the cancer of over-bureaucratisation – 'paper everywhere, decisions nowhere' – but considered its worst evil the waste of academics' time. He allowed administrative and support staff to increase only pro rata with academic and related staff; expansion based on Parkinson's law was curtailed. Ashby's own office was frugal: in fact he had a sneaking nostalgia for the garret, candle and handwritten script, the last-named at least characterised his own early research submissions. Unencumbered by having to meet the insatiable demands of the modern state's *dirigisme* and the endless search for ever-increasing funds, one venerable secretary, access to the typing pool, an occasional part-time typist and a temporary part-time research assistant met his considerable in-house and extra-mural requirements. He later lamented the rise of the 'strong' registrar; rather more perhaps the need for one.

VALEDICTION

By 1957 Ashby had led Queen's onto the national stage. It was the best of times but too good to last. That year he was nominated as a candidate for the mastership of Clare College, Cambridge; in early 1958 he was pre-elected master and in April 1959 he left Queen's. He had enjoyed Queen's and most certainly Queen's had enjoyed him. 'If I was asked on *Desert Island Discs* the appointment in my life I would put first,' he told an interviewer, 'I would say Chancellor of Queen's. It was the feeling that ... I was back among people who had liked me so much that they invited me to return.'[21] He was the unopposed nominee in 1970 for the chancellorship, an office he filled with distinction and (I know) more than a little pleasure. He was (I also know) of great assistance and a source of comfort to at least one subsequent vice-chancellor. In 1983 he retired from this office to enjoy his family, and his musical and intellectual interests; do the daily shopping (early morning was his preferred time) from his house in Cambridge or cottage in Brandon; lunch with Helen at Clare Hall; attend when possible the House of Lords where, as Baron Ashby of Brandon, Suffolk, he had sat on the cross benches since 1973 as a working peer; and keep up his meticulously conducted correspondence by laborious typing when his handwriting finally failed. He never complained and his later health problems remain privy to his doctors, family and a few close friends. He remained a humble, gracious and selfless man until his death on 22 October 1992. A memorial service was held at Great St Mary's, Cambridge, on 6 February 1993. Nothing speaks more eloquently of his international esteem than, among symbols of recognition, his twenty-four honorary degrees from universities in nine countries, numerous honorary memberships and fellowships from learned and professional societies, trusteeships, public and eponymous lectureships and visiting professorships worldwide, and more than a dozen books, some translated into several languages, as well as other publications too numerous to count.

ASSESSMENT

Ashby's contributions to Queen's are incalculable; in return Queen's supplied a microcosm of the challenges he would later face on a wider stage. He was unarguably one of the great university leaders and educationalists of the last century. Inevitably he had his critics, mostly the usual suspects among the jealous and envious and the holders of grudges, real or perceived. Some said that he was authoritarian, even autocratic (true, but he never strayed beyond constitutional limits), that he was an opportunist (also true, but not in a pejorative sense, only that he seized and capitalised on his opportunities), even that he was too image-conscious and publicity-seeking outside Queen's (not true; conspicuous, certainly, but not overly so given his institution's objectives and his bestriding, to everyone's advantage, the local scene by sheer ability, energy and personality). Above all, they said he was lucky. There is some substance in this. Certainly he often seemed to be in the right place at the right time: the tranquillity on campus and in society, Queen's monopoly of Northern Ireland's higher education supply and near monopoly of the local graduate elite, the collegiality, defined function and modest size of Queen's at a time when university autonomy in so many fields was real and not the fiction it later became – all of these factors allowed scope for an able man to stamp on the university his vision, personality and beliefs, which later circumstances would not allow. If he was fortunate in the times he was the right person to exploit them. (When similarly branded as 'lucky', the golfer Gary Player would retort 'Perhaps I am, but I always notice that the harder I practise the luckier I seem to get.') Napoleon famously noted that 'luck' is a vital ingredient of success, and not just in generals. I would prefer to say 'the absence of bad luck', and this certainly Ashby enjoyed.

EPILOGUE

The Oxford Dictionary of National Biography modestly subtitles Ashby's entry as 'botanist and university administrator'. It could justifiably have added 'higher education visionary', 'scientific missionary', 'environmentalist' and 'public scientist'. Queen's would also add 'inspirational leader'. What had been a small, under-funded and provincially orientated university in 1950 had by 1960 become a ranking national university with international reach. Ashby's term as vice-chancellor has proved to be one of the great masterclasses in British and Irish university history.

---

[1] Alan Burges and Richard J. Eden, 'Ashby, Eric: Baron Ashby (1904–1992), Botanist and University Administrator', *Oxford DNB*, (2004).

[2] Ashby's experiences in Moscow led to the first of his many acclaimed books, Eric Ashby, *Scientist in Russia* (Harmondsworth: Penguin Books, 1947).

[3] J. Heslop-Harrison, 'Eric Ashby, Baron Ashby, of Brandon, Suffolk, Kt. 24 August 1904–22 October 1992. Elected FRS 1963', *Biographical Memoirs of Fellows of the Royal Society* 41: 3–18 (1995): 3.

[4] For information on Ashby's earlier career I have relied on John Heslop-Harrison's memoir in *Biographical Memoirs* (1995), 3–18; Alan Burges and Richard Eden's article in the *Oxford DNB* (2004); obituaries in relevant periodicals (*The Times*, 29 October 1992; *Independent*, 28 and 30 Oct 1992, 5 and 28 November 1992); and sundry other sources. Details on Ashby's years at Queen's are drawn from Leslie Clarkson's *A University in Troubled Times: Queen's Belfast, 1945–2000* (Dublin: Four Courts Press, 2004); Brian Walker and Alf McCreary's *Degrees of Excellence: The Story of Queen's, Belfast, 1845–1995* (Belfast: Queen's University Belfast, Institute of Irish Studies, 1994); from Queen's archives and personal knowledge.

[5] Henrik Lundergårdh, *Klima und Boden in Ihrer Wirkung Auf das Pflanzenleben* (Jena: Verlag von Gustav Fischer, 1925); E. Ashby, *Environment and Plant Development*, translated and edited from the German of Henrik Lundergårdh by Eric Ashby (London: Edward Arnold, 1931); Helen Ashby, Eric Ashby, Harald Richter, Johannes Bärner and others, *German–English Botanical Terminology: An Introduction to German and English Terms Used in Botany Including Plant Physiology* (London: Murby, 1938).

[6] A fellow passenger was the twenty-five-year-old Enoch Powell en route to take the chair of Greek, also at the University of Sydney. He asked Ashby to save all letters which he, Powell, might write to him. Later he asked Ashby for their return for autobiographical purposes – and for posterity!

[7] He once suggested that, to avoid any clash of topics, we exchange drafts of our forthcoming (July) graduation addresses. His draft arrived in February; he got mine in June. The exercise was not repeated!

[8] Sir Reginald Palgrave, *The Chairman's Handbook: Suggestions and Rules for the Conduct of Chairmen of Public and Other Meetings Based upon the Procedure and the Practice of Parliament*, revised by G.F.M. Campion and L.A. Abraham (25th ed., London: J.M. Dent and Sons, 1937).

[9] The only occasion on which I saw him enraged was when a fellow dinner guest at my table discourteously (and incorrectly) suggested that my son's well-earned place at Clare College owed not a little to Ashby's influence as a previous master.

[10] I.T. Ker (ed.), *The Idea of a University, Defined and Illustrated, by John Henry Newman* (Oxford: Clarendon Press, 1976), xxiv. The book contains Newman's series of public lectures given in Dublin in 1852 augmented with his subsequent thoughts, and first published (in an abridged edition) in 1859.

[11] Vice-chancellor's Report, 1956–7, 164–5 (published as an appendix to the Senate Minutes for that year).

[12] *The Future of Higher Education in Northern Ireland* (Belfast: HMSO, 1982).

[13] *Higher Education in Northern Ireland: The Future Structure* (Belfast: HMSO, 1982).

[14] Ashby later co-authored a book on this subject – Eric Ashby and Mary Anderson, *Portrait of Haldane at Work on Education* (London: Macmillan, 1974).

[15] Eric Ashby, 'The Scientist as University President', *Arthur Holby Compton Memorial Lecture* (St Louis, Missouri: Washington University, 1965).

[16] 'Reminiscences of Lord Ashby of Brandon, 1990'. Quoted in Clarkson's *A University in Troubled Times* (2004), 19.

[17] Eric Ashby and Mary Anderson, *The Rise of the Student Estate in Britain* (London: Macmillan, 1970).

[18] *Investment in Education: Report of a Commission into Post-Secondary and Higher Education in Nigeria, 1959–1961* (New York: The Carnegie Foundation, 1962).

[19] Eric Ashby, *Technology and the Academics: An Essay on Universities in the Scientific Revolution* (London: Macmillan, 1958).

[20] Ashby told me how the wealthy Salt Lake City jeweller-cum-philanthropist Obert Tanner could not believe that an honorarium for his eponymous annual lecture of $10,000 could fail to produce twice as good a lecture as one of $5,000; after all (Tanner argued) it would buy twice as good a watch! Ashby considered that Belfast's commercial culture was more understanding than that in Utah.

[21] Cited in Walker and McCreary's *Degrees of Excellence*, 93.

E. Estyn Evans and the Interpretation of the Irish Landscape

HENRY GLASSIE

HENRY GLASSIE is College Professor of Folklore at Indiana University.

Emyr Estyn Evans (1905–1989) would have us begin geographically, in place, with Ireland, sea-girt and rimmed by broken mountains, an island made human by people who fished its edges and followed its eel-rich rivers inland, felling its forests to graze their cattle and dividing its manifest unity into four provinces and two halves, north and south, then east and west, then north and south again.[1]

For this island, broken by borders, Estyn Evans came prepared. He was born in Shrewsbury in 1905 to Welsh-speaking parents, and raised in the Welsh borderland. His revered mentor, H.J. Fleure, wrote that Evans's youth, in suspension between tamed England and wild Wales, enabled him to step aside and take an analytical angle, understanding the orderly villages of the arable lowlands and the lonely steadings of the pastoral uplands, while appreciating the mixed culture that flourishes along lines of division.[2] Evans went to Aberystwyth and studied geography and anthropology with Fleure, perfecting his bifocal perspective. Then in 1928, at the age of twenty-three, he accepted a lectureship at Queen's University, founding the department of geography, where he would serve for forty years – serve so effectively that at the department's golden jubilee in 1978, its academic staff had grown from one to twenty-one.[3]

When Estyn Evans came to Belfast and made Ireland his home, the cruel war was over, the new border was set, and he began his own campaign on the academic borders that split the university. While holding respect for differences, for the integrity of scholarly traditions, Evans worked for interdisciplinary cooperation and sought intellectual unity. He used geography as his base of operations, while fostering archaeology and anthropology at Queen's, and he strove throughout his career to combine geography, anthropology and history in the quest for a useful and democratic universal history of humankind.

In his profound capstone statement, *The Personality of Ireland*,[4] based on the Wiles Lectures given at Queen's in 1971, the words Evans used for his triad of humanistic endeavour were: habitat, heritage and history. The alliteration suited his elegant style, as did the exactitude with which he chose his words. Habitat is not mere geography, but an ecology of conditions for human existence. Heritage is the collective accumulation of experience and speculation that enables life in place. History is the pattern in time that follows the mutable merger of habitat and heritage. His goal was the production of an accurate and comprehensive understanding of the past, lived in the present, and full of hope for a future of peace and decency and human fulfilment. Professor Evans's prime inspiration was French. In 1937 he published a successful cultural geography of France[5] and throughout his writings he cited with pointed approval French historians: Fernand Braudel, with whom he shared a spatial orientation to civilization and an alertness to the long duration, and especially Marc Bloch, with whom he shared the great historian's gift of imagination and an understanding of rural labour and life.[6]

After his graduation from Aberystwyth, and recuperating from tuberculosis in Wiltshire, Evans worked as a field archaeologist. When he came to Ulster, he surveyed the prehistoric monuments, and during the 1930s he conducted a series of significant digs, culminating in his great success at the Neolithic site of Lyles Hill in County Antrim. His archaeological understanding, reported in *Prehistoric and Early Christian Ireland*, laid the firm foundation upon which he framed his view of Irish history.[7]

In bending to dig and standing to look over the windy, wet landscape, Evans witnessed the long succession of invasions: Mesolithic fisherfolk and knappers of flint, Neolithic potters and builders of bold stone tombs, Celtic warriors and herdsmen, Christian missionaries and agricultural innovators, Norse raiders and founders of cities, English planters and planners, hardworking Scots settlers – Irish, eventually, all of them.

The sequence bears little surprise, but his take was his own. The Irish landscape is a book of failed invasions. Every intrusion was incomplete: one after another, Ireland conquered her conquerors. Evans did not view history's sequence in the customary Western way as neatly segmented, a rising pile of sealed periods, but in the Japanese manner as cumulative. The pre-Celtic lingers in the Celtic, the pre-Christian in the Christian. Planter and Gael battle and blend. The past has not passed: the Irish landscape is a palimpsest, a vibrant simultaneity. In Irish life, as on the Irish land, shards from all the strata of the past commingle in a unity of diversity, of mixed races and hybrid culture. We are all mongrels, Prof. Evans liked to say, and he regularly exemplified the virtues of mongrelhood with the stunning wonder of twentieth-century Irish literature in English.[8]

For Evans, a cumulative impurity is the reality. In his history, continuity trumps change.[9] The prime cause of continuity lies in the habitat within which history necessarily unfolds. Ancient practices abide, survivals survive, because old and tested ideas continue to prove adaptive in the perduring predicament of the environment. It pleased Prof. Evans to quote J.C. Beckett, a great historian presented elsewhere in this collection by Alvin Jackson. 'The history of Ireland,' Beckett wrote, 'must be based on a study of the relationship between the land and the people. It is in Ireland itself ... that the historian will find the distinct and continuing character of Irish history.'[10]

A powerful sense of continuity turned Evans from one prehistory to another, from the prehistory of the grey megaliths to the prehistory of bally and booley and work with the spade – the rural life of Ireland that was prehistoric in the sense that it remained unwritten. Evans became the scribe of silence. On life in the country, he wrote two general books, *Irish Heritage* and *Irish Folk Ways*, masterpieces of folklife research, and he wrote the best of all local studies, *Mourne Country*.[11]

Astonishing change on the land since Evans's day makes shocking his bold assertion that Ireland is a land of peasants.[12] The usual academic view centres national life among rich men in the cities and leaves country people at the forgettable edge. But Evans had the courage to overturn convention and locate Ireland's centre among the historical majority. The people of Ireland were peasants who farmed, growing oats for bread and thatching material, but they were primarily stockmen, herders of cattle. Topography, soil and climate – hills, clay and rain – combined to make Ireland a pastoral place. And pastoral action shaped in the mind a culture of independence and kin ties, of nimble risks, of lawlessness, not civic compliance. In the long dialectic of location and culture, of habitat and heritage, the Irish landscape became a scatter of white houses, set separately among their green fields. Its pastoral people did not put their energies into the fragile and fine – there were no ceramics to match China's, no polished oak furniture to match that of Wales. Irish crafts were pragmatic and plain; Irish arts were verbal and individualistic. Ireland became a place of separate farms, of taciturn workers and garrulous characters, of rebels, poets and solo singers.[13]

Prof. Evans revealed the sincerity of his belief in the signal conjunction of pastoralism and independence by the way he mounted the same argument in writings different in scope. He told the story at the local level in Antrim and Down, at the provincial level in Ulster, at the level of the whole island of Ireland, and at the wide regional level when he positioned Ireland with Spain, with Wales and Scotland, with Norway, in a grand Atlantic realm, united by maritime connections, environmental conditions and a consistency of human response.

His own places – Wales, southwestern England and Ireland, north and south – joined in Evans's Atlantic region.[14] Then he stood in Ireland, the western outpost of the Atlantic fringe, and sought still wider connections. He looked east to the end of the Indo-European domain and compared the social orders of India and Celtic Ireland. He looked west along the routes of migration to the New World, where the Ulster-Scots became the Scotch-Irish, hacking farms out of the Appalachian forests and creating a dispersed, highland landscape like Ireland's. And searching yet further, Evans used his anthropological reading to sprinkle his prose with surprising comparisons, with cultural parallels from the far ends of Africa and Asia that overleapt crude evolutionary disjunctions, sidestepped divisions of race, and linked little Ireland to all of the world.

Prof. Evans at once saw the big picture and loved its tiny details. He had the courage to generalise provocatively, and the courage to invite contradiction and complexity into his view. Ireland is a land of peasants, he wrote, and then he wrote about urban development and industrialisation. Belfast was his place as much as the glens of Antrim.[15] Pastoral Ireland spreads with independent farmsteads. It contrasts with the orderly landscape of village England, providing a geographical basis for perpetual misunderstanding. Then immediately he undermines his dualistic scheme by emphasising the clachan, the compressed hamlet with its open-field rundale system.

The clachan lies in concept between the poles of the farmstead and village, making Evans's Ireland a place of neighbourliness as well as independence, of cordial ceilidhs and cooperative work in the bog, as well as herding the damned old cows.[16] His view complicates toward the conclusion reached by Æ– what makes Ireland distinct is a simultaneous, paradoxical valuing of the individual and the communal.[17]

In his writing, habitat and heritage unify Ireland and split Ireland apart. Everywhere the old farmhouses were whitewashed and thatched, low, narrow and long. But an angled line, scored on the map from northeast to southwest, separated houses by their floor-plans, signalling different spheres of influence – an Ireland of the east with its connections to England, an Ireland of the west with its connections to Scotland.[18]

Ireland is one, a green smear in the ocean, but a swag of drumlins sunders the north from the south. In megalithic times, the drumlins marked a religious divide, foreshadowing the border that had been drawn through the low hills of glacial drift shortly before Evans arrived to make Ireland his home and his topic.[19]

In the words Jean-Paul Sartre set before us in a late essay, E. Estyn Evans was skilled and disciplined, but no technician.[20] He was, in the best sense of the word, an amateur, ready to break the chains of convention and face the complexities. He was an intellectual.

As an intellectual, Evans worked for interdisciplinary union, and he gracefully crossed the border that divided the academic from the popular. Committed to public education, Evans used the radio and television to gain a wide audience, and he assumed a crucial role of leadership in the creation of the Ulster Folk and Transport Museum.[21] The museum at Cultra sets before the people an image of the unity and complexity of Ulster, and it stands, through his work and the work of his students, as one of the finest open-air museums in the world.

Evans crossed a still deeper divide, bringing serious science into unity with serious art. His publications are illustrated with his own fine drawings. His meticulous field notes are filled with accurate and artful pen sketches and lovely little watercolours. Gwyneth, his wonderful wife, wrote that within her handsome husband, 'there was a poet struggling to break free'.[22] He had a poet's way with words, a pulling of feeling into their arrangement, and an Irish poet's love for the land, its shifting light and windy prospects, its history sunken into small things. But Evans himself felt there was a novelist inside him,[23] and he was the kinsman of novelists like the Melville of *Moby-Dick*, who honoured empirical precision, sought the company of hardworking people, and showed respect for their readers in a language never academical, never too simple, but cadenced, engaging and hewn to the true.

An intellectual, a scientist and an artist, Evans was all of a man – a husband, a father of successful sons, a generous and loyal friend, a teacher so revered that his students spoke of him as The Prof., as though there were no other. They honoured him with four Festschrifts, and they – John Mogey, G.B. Thompson, Alan Gailey, Bruce Proudfoot, Rosemary Harris, Ronald H. Buchanan, Desmond McCourt – honoured him even more by continuing his line of work, upon the Irish land, and with the Irish people.

Before his death in 1989, Estyn Evans had received major awards from geographical societies on both sides of the Atlantic, and he had become the great interpreter of the Irish landscape, a world leader in studies of archaeology, folklife and geography, a rare hero for the fractured modern academy.

---

[1] The invitation to speak about my friend and master Estyn Evans provided me with a marvellous opportunity to read again his writings, and after reading them in sequence, I wrote to evoke the themes in his oeuvre, employing his key words to compose my homage.

[2] H. J. Fleure, 'Emyr Estyn Evans: A Personal Note', in Ronald H. Buchanan, Emrys Jones and Desmond McCourt, eds, *Man and His Habitat: Essays Presented to Emyr Estyn Evans* (London: Routledge and Kegan Paul, 1971), 1–7, especially 2.

[3] The best biographical source is Gwyneth Evans, 'Estyn: A Biographical Memoir', in E. Estyn Evans, *Ireland and the Atlantic Heritage: Selected Writings* (Dublin: Lilliput Press, 1996), 1–19. Also: J. A. Campbell, *The Queen's University of Belfast Department of Geography Jubilee, 1928–1978* (Belfast: Department of Geography, Queen's University, 1978), 45.

[4] E. Estyn Evans, *The Personality of Ireland: Habitat, Heritage and History* (Cambridge: Cambridge University Press, 1973).

5 E. Estyn Evans, *France: A Geographical Introduction* (London: Christophers, 1937).
6 See Evans, *Personality of Ireland*, 10–11, 67, 72, 84.
7 E. Estyn Evans, *Lyles Hill: A Late Neolithic Site in County Antrim* (Archaeological and Research Publications [NI], Belfast: Her Majesty's Stationery Office, 1953); E. Estyn Evans, *Prehistoric and Early Christian Ireland: A Guide* (London: B. T. Batsford, 1966).
8 See Evans, *Irish and the Atlantic Heritage*, 33, 162–6.
9 See Evans, *Personality of Ireland*, 16–17, 47–8.
10 Evans, *Personality of Ireland*, 16; Evans, *Ireland and the Atlantic Heritage*, 32.
11 E. Estyn Evans, *Irish Heritage: The Landscape, The People and Their Work* (Dundalk: Dundalgan Press, 1951); E. Estyn Evans, *Irish Folk Ways* (London: Routledge and Kegan Paul, 1957); E. Estyn Evans, *Mourne Country: Landscape and Life in South Down* (1951; reprint, Dundalk: Dundalgan Press, 1967).
12 Evans, *Irish Heritage*, 10; Evans, *Ireland and the Atlantic Heritage*, 42.
13 See E. Estyn Evans, *Northern Ireland* (London: Collins, 1951), 10, 30, 48–9, 61; Evans, *Irish Heritage*, 7–13, 36–7, 47; Evans, *Irish Folk Ways*, 8–12, 20–1; Evans, *Personality of Ireland*, 38–40, 53–60, 69, 73–5; Evans, *Ireland and the Atlantic Heritage*, 32, 40, 43, 50–5, 56–62, 69–72, 165–70.
14 See Evans, *Irish Heritage*, 7–9; Evans, *Ireland and the Atlantic Heritage*, 59–73.
15 See E. Estyn Evans, ed., *Belfast in Its Regional Setting: A Scientific Survey* (Belfast: British Association for the Advancement of Science, 1952).
16 See Evans, *Mourne Country*, 122–3; Evans, *Northern Ireland*, 48–9; Evans, *Irish Heritage*, 47–52; Evans, *Irish Folk Ways*, 9–10, 21–6, 30–4; Evans, *Personality of Ireland*, 53–62; and E. Estyn Evans, 'Introduction' to *Facts from Gweedore Compiled from the Notes of Lord George Hill*, MRIA Institute of Irish Studies, 1 (1887; reprint, Belfast: Queen's University Institute of Irish Studies, 1971).
17 Æ [George Russell], *The National Being: Some Thoughts on an Irish Polity* (1916; reprint, New York: Macmillan, 1930), 124–31.
18 E. Estyn Evans, 'The Ulster Farmhouse', *Ulster Folklife* 1 (1955), 27–31; Evans, *Irish Heritage*, chapter 7; Evans, *Irish Folk Ways*, chapter 4; Evans, *Personality of Ireland*, 54, 62–5.
19 See Evans, *Personality of Ireland*, 72.
20 See Jean-Paul Sartre, *Between Existentialism and Marxism* (New York: William Morrow, 1974), 228–85.
21 See G. B. Thompson, 'Estyn Evans and the Development of the Ulster Folk Museum', in the Festschrift for Evans edited by Desmond McCourt and Alan Gailey, *Ulster Folklife* 15/16 (1970): 233–8.
22 Gwyneth Evans, 'Estyn', in Evans, *Ireland and the Atlantic Heritage*, 1.
23 Evans, *Ireland and the Atlantic Heritage*, 222.

David Robert Bates and the Belfast School of Physics

ALEXANDER DALGARNO

ALEX DALGARNO is Phillips Professor of Astronomy at Harvard University.

David Bates (1916–1994) was appointed professor and head of the department of applied mathematics at Queen's in 1951.[1] After graduating at Queen's with first-class honours in both experimental physics and mathematical physics in 1938 he obtained an MSc degree under the supervision of Harrie Massey. In the following year Massey, who occupied the position at Queen's of special lecturer in theoretical physics, was appointed to the Goldschmid chair of applied mathematics at University College London and he took with him his exceptionally talented student, David Bates. The war interrupted their research plans, though they did succeed in writing two papers relating to the physics of the ionosphere. The structure of the ionosphere was to have been the central topic of Bates's PhD thesis, which he never did complete.

With the end of the war Bates returned to University College London as a member of the faculty, initially in the department of applied mathematics and subsequently in the department of physics, when Massey was appointed as its head. Bates collaborated with Massey in studies of the ionosphere, which Bates extended to a comprehensive investigation of the energetics, dynamics, radiation and chemistry of the terrestrial atmosphere. In so doing a new discipline was created which we now call aeronomy. It identifies the physical, dynamical and chemical processes that occur when an atmosphere is subjected to radiation from a parent star and sets up equations that relate the production and loss mechanisms of the individual components of the system. The equations can be solved numerically and the consequences can be compared with observations. The original assumptions can then be modified to achieve consistency. Considerable physical insight is needed to discover the possible mechanisms and the conclusions often have implications well beyond the specific circumstances.

I will give you an example. Bates found there was a persistent discrepancy between the theoretical model and radio measurements of electron densities in the atmosphere. It led him to invent a process called dissociative recombination. As a process, it was not excluded on fundamental grounds but it seemed implausible. In a brilliant insight made after long consideration, Bates understood how it could proceed, how it would depend on the system and why it would usually be a rapid process. The process is now recognised as the major electron removal process in all low-temperature plasmas, atmospheric, astrophysical and technological. Because of its wide-ranging applicability a conference is held every two years devoted to the continued exploration of dissociative recombination.

At University College London, Bates also began his programme of fundamental research on the development of methods of quantum mechanics and their application to the prediction of the properties of atoms and molecules, which was to become a focus of the research at Queen's.

The invitation to Bates to head the department of applied mathematics at Queen's was extended, I was told, by a very hesitant administration, but turned out to be inspired. Bates was devoted to the welfare of Northern Ireland and all its people and despite many invitations to join more renowned institutions he remained at Queen's for the rest of his life.

Bates arrived in Belfast in 1951 to find a department that had been barely surviving since the departure of the distinguished theoretical physicist Professor P.P. Ewald to the United States. It survived only because of the heroic efforts of John Herivel, who was a lecturer, indeed the lecturer, in the department. The undergraduate teaching was onerous, though compensated for somewhat by the presence of some exceptionally able students from the local schools who were well trained in basic mathematics and physics. Bates immediately established a postgraduate programme, and after they graduated many of the students were eager to explore this new opportunity to conduct original research. It was, in my view, this combination of Bates, full of ideas for projects, and talented hard-working students (Bates made sure they were hard-working) that began and drove the evolution of the department of applied mathematics into the world-renowned centre for theoretical atomic, molecular and optical physics that it became and is today. Many of the students went on to occupy important academic and administrative positions in universities at home and abroad. Crucial to ensuring the continuing intellectual leadership of the centre was the additional appointment of creative faculty that Bates made then and through the following years as the department grew.

The department became a mecca and it attracted scholars from other institutions around the world. Two in particular come to mind: Professor James Browne of the University of Texas and Professor Neal Lane of the University of Oklahoma came as visiting scientists. I mention Neal Lane because he went on to become science advisor to President Bill Clinton in the United States. Jim Browne went from visiting scientist to professor of computing science at Queen's, a position that Bates persuaded the university to create. The appointment heralded the expansion of electronic computation in which Queen's is today a major force. The department of computer science became a separate entity but the introduction of computer science and technology to Queen's was triggered by the acquisition of an electronic digital computing machine for the department of applied mathematics. Bates's research activities had attracted the attention of the Office of Scientific Research of the United States Air Force and Bates obtained from it the necessary funding. Many at Queen's responded to the opportunity. I recall that Sir Peter Froggatt was one of the earliest users from outside the department of applied mathematics. The machine generated a lot of heat and the building in which it was housed was a warm, popular gathering place in the Belfast winters.

Working with the visiting scientists, graduate students and postdoctoral fellows, Bates did monumental research into the processes of atomic, molecular and optical physics.[2] His range was awesome and he had a deep understanding of physical mechanisms. He often appeared to know the outcome of a particular avenue of research before it had been reached. Bates used his immense knowledge and creative insight to uncover the origin of atmospheric phenomena and to predict the response of the atmosphere to natural and man-made perturbations. He was early in drawing attention to the hazards of industrial and agricultural pollution. His was more than a voice of concern. He supported his opinions with quantitative calculations of processes and their consequences. With Agnes Witherspoon, a graduate student, and Paul Hays, a visiting scientist, Bates showed that minor constituents had major effects. He pointed to the role of micro-organisms as sources and sinks and discussed the influence of oil wells, internal combustion engines, coal mines and the combustion of solid fuels. Bates put forward powerful arguments, drew reasoned conclusions and offered balanced judgments.[3] His conceptual approach has been widely adopted. Research on atmospheric science was recognised belatedly by the award, in 1995, of the Nobel Prize in chemistry to three distinguished researchers. The work for which they were honoured derives directly from seminal papers written by Bates who, had he been alive at the time, would surely have been a recipient of the prize.

Bates used the same methodology to attack the problem of explaining the observed abundances of interstellar molecules. In a collaboration with Lyman Spitzer at Princeton, who provided a model of the physical environment, Bates identified the formation and destruction processes and carried out calculations of the rates of the reactions, much as he had done for the terrestrial atmosphere. His approach is the basis today of the extensive studies, now in progress, of molecules in astrophysical environments from the early universe to the atmospheres of extrasolar planets.

The department of physics at Queen's has grown in parallel and has come to occupy a similar position of excellence. Physics and applied and pure mathematics now jointly form a school. The development of the physics department was greatly influenced by Bates's presence, which was important, not least, in helping to attract distinguished experimenters to Queen's. The basis for the growth of experimental physics was laid by Professor George Emeleus, who conducted pioneering research on the physics of gas discharges, what we would call gaseous electronics today. When Bates entered Queen's as an undergraduate it was his intention to concentrate on chemistry. It was the lectures of Professor Emeleus that inspired David Bates to take up physics. David was also attracted into physics by Dr Robert Harvey Sloane, who was carrying out innovative, ingenious experiments and obtaining remarkable results on the production of negative ions from beams of positive ions impacting surfaces. His discoveries, to be repeated much later by others, went largely unrecognised because of his reluctance to tell anyone about his results. I remember that he would occasionally tell me about some intriguing effect he had found but only if I would first promise not to tell anyone else. Nevertheless the positive atmosphere generated by an ongoing active research programme was a great stimulus to Bates.

Perhaps unexpectedly, given his commitment to science and education and his devotion to his family, Bates emerged as an influential, eloquent voice, leading the university's protest at the invasion of Hungary in 1956 by forces of the Soviet Union. Over a decade later, Bates was deeply distressed by the violence in Northern Ireland and participated actively in the establishment of the non-sectarian Alliance Party, of which he was a vice-president.

Bates received many honours in the form of medals, prizes, honorary degrees and memberships of prestigious societies. He was elected a fellow of the Royal Society and a member of the Royal Irish Academy, the Académie Royale de Belgique, the American Academy of Arts and Sciences and the United States National Academy of Sciences. For his service to science and education he was knighted in 1978.

Let me close on a more personal note. David Bates was more than a great scientist. He was a warm, encouraging, sometimes demanding mentor, deeply engaged in trying to ensure that his students did not fail to realise their full potential. It was good to be able to call him a friend. Together Sir David and Lady Bates were the heart of an extended international family of students, visiting scholars, post-doctoral fellows and faculty members bound together in productive interaction by their affection and respect for David and Barbara. Queen's is greatly indebted to both of them.[4]

---

[1] David Bates published 337 papers in more than ten different scientific journals. A compete listing can be obtained from the Royal Society Library.
[2] David Bates ed., *Atomic and Molecular Processes* (New York and London: Academic Press, 1962).
[3] David Bates ed., *Quantum Mechanics Vols I, II and III* (New York and London: Academic Press, 1962).
[4] For further reading see Benjamin Bederson and Alexander Dalgarno eds, *Advances in Atomic, Molecular and Optical Physics: Vol. 32* (US: Academic Press Inc., 1994).

J.C. Beckett and the Making of Modern Irish Historiography

ALVIN JACKSON

ALVIN JACKSON is Sir Richard Lodge Professor of History at the University of Edinburgh.

I

Irish historiography in the early twentieth century was heavily influenced by the two dominating political traditions on the island, revolutionary separatism and Ulster unionism. In the 1930s a new generation of Irish historians, who had reached adulthood in the aftermath of partition and revolution, embarked upon a series of reforms, creating new institutions within which an ostensibly more 'scientific' historical methodology might be practised, and seeking to liberate the discipline from the constraints of politics. Belfast, and Queen's University, were focuses of this enterprise. There were certainly other critical laboratories for this 'new' history, such as the Institute of Historical Research in London; there were also other critical players, primarily Robin Dudley Edwards, who in 1945 became professor of modern Irish history at University College Dublin. But Belfast was undeniably significant, and the reasons for this merit some investigation.

Among the protagonists of the new history were J.C. Beckett, R.B. McDowell, T.W. Moody and D.B. Quinn, who were all born in the immediate prelude to the Irish revolution, who all shared lower-middle-class or working-class origins, and who were all (with the exception of McDowell) educated at Queen's University Belfast. The three Queen's graduates benefited from the bracingly analytical approaches pursued in the department of history by its successive professors, Maurice Powicke (see Chapter 7, 'Maurice Powicke: Medieval Historical Scholarship and Queen's') and James Eadie Todd. All four were young enough to escape some of the political chauvinism prevalent at the time of the creation of the two Irish states. Though they were all Protestant, they were not all unionist; nor were they sufficiently well placed (in terms of social background) to be counted among the beneficiaries of partition and of the Stormont regime. Their lives spanned the boundary between a unified and a divided Ireland, both in a chronological and a spatial sense: all were born before partition, and the careers of McDowell, Moody and Quinn were played out on both sides of the border. All of the group retained a very strong sense of the cultural unity of Ireland, and all were highly sensitive to exclusivist and tendentious readings of the island's history, including those of the partitionist variety.

Beckett, Moody and Quinn each taught Irish history at Queen's (Moody between 1935 and 1939, and Quinn between 1939 and 1944), but it was Beckett who retained the strongest connections with the university. Beckett graduated in history from Queen's in 1934, studied for an MA under Moody, and lectured in the Queen's history department from 1945 until 1975. There he published the work upon which his subsequent celebrity was founded: *Protestant Dissent in Ireland, 1687–1780* (London: Faber & Faber, 1948), *A Short History of Ireland* (London: Hutchinson, 1952), *The Making of Modern Ireland* (London: Faber & Faber, 1966), *Confrontations: Studies in Irish History* (London: Faber & Faber, 1972). He and Moody chronicled the history of the university in *Queen's, Belfast, 1845–1949: The History of a University* (2 vols, London: Faber & Faber, 1959). After retirement in 1975 Beckett published two intensely personal studies, *The Anglo-Irish Tradition* (London: Faber & Faber, 1976), which he regarded as his masterpiece, and *The Cavalier Duke: A Life of James Butler, 1st Duke of Ormond* (Belfast: Pretani Press, 1990). He ended his career as professor of Irish history, a member of the Royal Irish Academy, and the recipient of several honorary doctorates.

II

The reformers of the 1930s were led by Moody of Queen's and Dudley Edwards of University College Dublin, but there were a number of important lieutenants, slightly younger, of whom Beckett was one. These men sought to redirect Irish history away from some of its more polemical adventures back to a rigorously documented and transparently source-based model which would avoid the uncertainties of contemporary controversy. Their manifesto, which was laid out as the preface to a new journal, *Irish Historical Studies*, in 1938, emphasised scientific rigour, the exploitation and discovery of new sources, and communication between scholars and the wider interested public, particularly those connected with the school system. They had an evangelical impulse: new institutions were created to forward this vision of the discipline, and Moody even went so far as to prescribe a uniform and exact system of presenting work for publication, designed originally for his and Dudley Edwards's new journal, but later more widely applied. They created societies in Belfast and Dublin to spread the word of the new faith, the Ulster Society for Irish Historical Studies and the Irish Historical Society; they founded a monograph series, Studies in Irish History, published by Faber & Faber in London, which was designed to publish the best book-length studies produced under the new regime. Later Moody promoted a vision of a massive synopsis of Irish history, the 'New History of Ireland', designed to be as nearly definitive as possible, and to encapsulate in detail the state of the Irish historiographical art.

Beckett was an essential part of this broad enterprise, and he was unquestionably important as an early proponent of the 'new' history. He was close to Moody throughout his professional career, and was active in the new societies founded by the reformers. He was a relatively frequent contributor to the new journal, *Irish Historical Studies*, both as a reviewer and as a writer of articles: his MA thesis was published as the second volume in the Faber monograph series under the title *Protestant Dissent in Ireland, 1687–1780*. He cooperated with Moody on numerous projects, including radio series, the history of Queen's (1959) and the New History of Ireland series.

However, Beckett's significance arises not only from his role as a reformer, but also – critically – from the fact that he took the best from the reforming agenda without ever succumbing to its potential for dogmatism: 'moderation', indeed, is the hallmark of Beckett's historical thought. The 'new history' of this period has been occasionally represented as a doctrinaire piece of professionalisation, or as an exercise in liberal dogmatism, by some of its critics. But Beckett can be seen as one of the more cautious of the young scholars struggling, in the 1930s, to respond to the variety of current and conflicting historical epistemologies. Like other moderate and reflective historians of the time, he sought to negotiate a path between the challenges posed by contemporary historicist, empiricist, patriotic and teleological readings of the past.

He actively promoted a rigorous, source-based historical

methodology; but in some ways he was a less austere practitioner than his fellow reformers of the 1930s. Despite their desire to reach out to the public, they have been criticised for their aridity and remoteness: Aidan Clarke has written cruelly of Moody's *The Londonderry Plantation, 1609–41* (Belfast: Mullan, 1939) that after the early pages 'it betrays no signs of human origin'.[1] Beckett, however, sought to combine a professional methodology with accessibility; and he built effective connections between the academic practice of Irish history and the wider community through a skilful use of the media, and through the most popular of his many works, *A Short History of Ireland* and *The Making of Modern Ireland*. These remain amongst the most highly successful and widely read surveys on modern Irish history, and they underline the extent of Beckett's influence on his discipline. But Beckett was also a frequent contributor to the press on historical issues, and a frequent contributor to radio programmes in the 1950s and 1960s. He was the architect, with Moody, of two very successful radio series on Irish history in the mid-1950s (later published as *Ulster Since 1800: A Political and Economic Survey* [London: BBC, 1954] and *Ulster Since 1800: A Social Survey* [London: BBC, 1957)]; he and R.E. Glasscock co-edited a radio series devoted to the history of Belfast (published as *Belfast: Origins and Growth of an Industrial City* [Belfast: BBC, 1967]). In Irish terms, Beckett was a relatively early public academic, or media don.

Beckett was closely associated with Moody and other reformers within the Irish historical profession of the 1930s; but he had also, perhaps, a stronger sense than his fellow 'revisionists' of the limitations and subjectivities of the discipline. Beckett certainly subscribed to the rigorous methodology which Moody and Edwards championed (the adjective 'scientific' occurs time and again in the reforming literature of the 1930s); but (as is evident in his most acutely personal work, *The Anglo-Irish Tradition*) Beckett's first scholarly love was literature, and it is arguable that he saw an artistic dimension to history – even if he accepted that the artist should employ rigorous techniques to achieve his or her ends.[2] It is arguable, too, that Beckett had a more lively historical imagination and empathy than many of his fellow 'revisionists' of the 1930s. It may be contended that he cared more about literary style, and more about the accessibility of his work, than his peers.

Just as in his intense religious faith Beckett accepted the innate sinfulness of man, so in his professional life he accepted the inevitable susceptibility of the historian. In different radio broadcasts in the mid-1950s Beckett underlined his distance from any doctrinaire scientism: speaking in 1954, he emphasised his conviction that 'no historian is infallible. I would go further, and say that no historian is completely impartial – no matter how scrupulous he is, there are presuppositions that he cannot get rid of.'[3] Speaking in 1956, Beckett reaffirmed that 'no historian, however careful and scrupulous he may be, is completely unbiased'.[4] In his inaugural lecture of 1963, 'The Study of Irish History', Beckett argued that 'the writing of history can never be simply teleological; it is influenced, but not governed, by the end which it serves; the process is more important than the conclusion'.[5] But there is ambiguity, or perhaps latitude, here, as elsewhere in Beckett's historiographical reflections: he is clearly prepared to accept that historical scholarship may, in fact, be 'influenced ... by the end which it serves'. Indeed, Beckett himself betrays a measure of contemporary preoccupation and influence by emphasising (in his *Short History of Ireland*) his concern to 'make the present situation intelligible by showing how it arose'.[6] There is also a mildly historicist inflection to the concluding argument of Beckett's masterpiece, *The Making of Modern Ireland*, where he seems to hint that the constitutional arrangements of the early 1920s had brought a form of 'end' to Irish history:'[T]hough the settlement left a legacy of bitterness, issuing occasionally in local and sporadic disturbances, it inaugurated for Ireland a longer period of general tranquillity than she had known since the first half of the eighteenth century.'[7] In any event, there is no question that here, or indeed elsewhere, Beckett evinced any absolute faith in a completely disinterested, still less a fully 'scientific' history.

In his lecture on 'The Study of Irish History' Beckett seeks to define the very nature of his discipline. He asks, bluntly, 'do we know what Irish history is about?' and works at length to supply an answer to his own question. Irish history evidently is 'about' the waves of settlement, the interactions of successive settlers with the natives, and the interaction of the entire community with the land: '[I]t is in Ireland itself, the physical conditions imposed by life in this country, and their effect on those who have lived here, that [the historian] will find the distinct and continuing character of Irish history.'[8] Elsewhere Beckett warns against 'the simplifying influence of theories', and 'an over-eager application of English parallels to Irish history'.[9] He is confident that there is an obvious 'hierarchy of importance in national histories'.[10] He is confident, too, that 'there is in English history a natural and recognisable pattern': the history of England, he declares, is a 'well-mapped country'.[11] But despite (in this argument) the relative importance of English history, and despite the historic interconnections between England and Ireland, Irish history is much more than the history of the Anglo-Irish relationship, and utterly distinct from (what Beckett defines as) the model of English historical development.[12] Beckett, thus, moved swiftly to defend the essential integrity and autonomy of Irish history.

In a sense, Beckett might well be seen as embodying a familiar paradox, being at once an empiricist, however 'moderate', and at the same time denying any ideological commitment. He argued, in prefacing his *Short History of Ireland* (1952), that he had 'no theory to vindicate, no policy to defend'; yet at the end of the same passage, he wrote that he had 'refused to define the term "Irish" in any narrow racial or linguistic sense, and [had] tried to write a history of the whole country'.[13] His definition of his subject in 'The Study of Irish History' is an elaboration of the same idea, and is deliberately pitted against notions of political exclusivism.[14] But, in writing these words, Beckett was clearly 'vindicating' a theory and 'defending' a policy: he was advocating an inclusivist vision of Irishness against what he saw as chauvinist alternatives.

III

Beckett affected a mild despair at the state of the modern world, but he was in many ways an intensely modern figure. He abhorred revolution, but has been identified as a kind of historiographical revolutionary, active in promoting far-reaching change in the discipline. As discussed, he was one of the patriarchs of the 'new' Irish history propagated in the 1930s which promoted rigorously source-based, cautious and disinterested scholarship. He was active in the main organs of this new enterprise, the societies, the journal and the monograph series. Loyal to the evangelising mission of the reformers, he was one of the first media dons on the island, active in newsprint and on the airwaves of the BBC. His central scholarly achievement, *The Making of Modern Ireland*, was groundbreaking – not because it was the first general history of Ireland by an academic – but because it was a brilliantly accessible summary of the achievements of a critical generation of Irish historians. He was not the first Irish historian at Queen's – Moody and Quinn both taught Irish history before Beckett was appointed in 1945 – but he had by far the longest tenure; and he was therefore a critical influence on several generations of history graduates, and indeed on the wider teaching of Irish history in these islands.

Some aspects of his historical thought and preoccupations, and in particular his celebration of the Anglo-Irish, appear dated or eccentric by contemporary standards. But if Beckett occasionally got his sums wrong, then the method of his calculations invariably makes sense; his celebration of the Anglo-Irish appeared wrong-headed to many, but it was rooted in a desire to explore the varieties of Irishness, and to identify cultural common ground in the partitioned and polarised Ireland of the 1970s. His concern for historical accuracy, his caution, his scepticism and his interest in the wider communication of his scholarship have all served to preserve his influence. He participated centrally in the reform of his discipline, but knew the limits of what was possible, and was profoundly wary of the appeal and dogmatism of scholarly fashion. His religiosity, which might easily have alienated his audience or dated his work, was implicit rather than overt; and it helped to preserve him from entanglement in other, inevitably transient, historical ideologies and approaches. In fact, paradoxically, his concern for religion and his empathy for religious mentalities have a curiously modern feel. But aside from, or perhaps because of, his religiosity, he was a natural centrist or mediator. Born and bred in the context of revolution, he had some experience of political passion and violence, and he preserved his distance. His instincts were inclusive – to negotiate between extremes, to chart the narrow ground of shared experience, to embrace, to communicate. Beckett's passion for moderation speaks to the new millennium.

1. Aidan Clarke, 'Robert Dudley Edwards (1909–1988)', *Irish Historical Studies* xxvi (1988–9), 121.
2. For the 'new historians' and scientific history see the manifesto for the Ulster Society for Irish Historical Studies (*c.* 1939) (University College Dublin [UCD] Archives Dudley Edwards Papers, LA22/390/70), the constitution of the Irish Historical Society, 14 July 1937 (UCD Archives Dudley Edwards Papers, LA22/3/92/2), and the prospectus for *Irish Historical Studies* (*c.* 1938) (UCD Archives Dudley Edwards Papers, LA22/849/30).
3. J.C. Beckett, 'The Eighteenth Century Background', in *Ulster Since 1800: A Political and Economic Survey: Twelve Talks Broadcast in the Northern Ireland Home Service of the BBC*, ed. T.W. Moody and J.C. Beckett (London: BBC, 1955), 10.
4. J.C. Beckett, 'Ulster before 1800', in *Ulster Since 1800, Second Series: A Social Survey: Twenty-two Talks Broadcast in the Northern Ireland Home Service of the BBC*, ed. T.W. Moody and J.C. Beckett (London: BBC, 1957), 18.
5. J.C. Beckett, 'The Study of Irish History: An Inaugural Lecture', in *Confrontations: Studies in Irish History* (London: Faber & Faber, 1972), 15–16.
6. J.C. Beckett, *A Short History of Ireland*, 6th ed. (London: Century Hutchinson, 1979), 7.
7. J.C. Beckett, *The Making of Modern Ireland, 1603–1923* (London: Faber & Faber, 1966).
8. Beckett, *Confrontations*, 12, 23.
9. J.C. Beckett, *Protestant Dissent in Ireland 1687–1780* (London: Faber & Faber, 1948), 13; Beckett, *Confrontations*, 22.
10. Beckett, *Confrontations*, 13–14.
11. Ibid., 14.
12. Ibid., 19–20, 22.
13. Beckett, *Short History*, 7.
14. Beckett, *Confrontations*, 23: 'To the Gaelic nationalist, the settlers may remain foreign invaders, an English garrison; but to the historian they are as much part of the Irish scene as the lands they conquered, the castles they built, the institutions they imported or devised.'

John Blacking and Ethnomusicology

MARTIN STOKES

MARTIN STOKES is University Lecturer in Ethnomusicology and Tutorial Fellow of Music at St John's College, Oxford.

Ethnomusicology is the study of music in culture and society. Its roots are deeply buried in the philosophical musings that accompanied early modern colonial expansion and European romanticism. It attained disciplinary focus with German systematic and comparative musicology in the later nineteenth century, in European folklore studies and in the cultural anthropology of Franz Boas in America in the early twentieth century. Increasingly, ethnomusicology has involved the study of a music culture not one's own. Like Philip Larkin (as Edna Longley suggests elsewhere in this volume), ethnomusicologists, too, need their 'elsewhere', to break ingrained habits of thought, and to gain the broadest possible perspective on human music making.

John Blacking (1928–1990) played a central role in creating the modern, professional, academic discipline of ethnomusicology. He received his education at Sherborne School, Dorset, and King's College, Cambridge. His long association with South Africa began with an invitation from Hugh Tracey in 1953 to work as resident musicologist at the International Library of African Music in that country. He carried out fieldwork amongst the Venda of the Northern Transvaal between 1956 and 1958, and took up a lectureship in social anthropology at the University of Witwatersrand in 1959. An energetic opponent of apartheid, he left South Africa, *persona non grata*, in 1969. He was appointed professor and chair of the newly established department of social anthropology at Queen's University Belfast that year, a post he held until his early death in 1990. In a string of highly influential books – *Venda Children's Songs* (1967), *How Musical Is Man?* (1973), *The Anthropology of The Body* (1977) and *A Common Sense View of All Music* (1987)[1] – Blacking advocated a simple but compelling thesis that he developed throughout his career. This is that music comprises a core modelling system for expressive behaviour, thought and sociality, that it is a universal human capacity, however it is culturally realised, and that the study of music can provide vital insight into processes of social and political transformation.

What does it mean to recall his legacy at this point in time? It is to join many others for a start. Blacking's memory has been well served by obituaries in national newspapers and professional journals, posthumously published interviews, edited collections and websites, and memorial lectures, conferences and concerts.[2] These have been informed by shock and grief at his sudden passing, a sense of work left undone, anxiety about the future for a fledgling discipline, nostalgia for an age of radicalism and experimentalism in the humanities and social sciences in European and American universities – an age that now seems, in some ways, remote. I have learned a great deal from such publications, events and occasions about the contexts that shaped and informed Blacking and his ethnomusicology, not having had the opportunity to get to know him as well as I would have liked in the one year I was at Queen's during his lifetime.[3]

He was undoubtedly the product of that wave of '-isms' that transformed social anthropology during his lifetime: structural-functionalism, Levi-Straussian structuralism, Chomskian linguistics, Marxism, feminism and transactionalism all shaped his writing and thinking in various ways. But he was also the product of a Tractarian family environment and early education, of Cambridge and the Coldstream Guards in the 1950s, and, most crucially of all, the counter-cultural dissent and the anti-colonial movements of the 1960s. It is in this combination of influences, ideas and experiences – very much those of the establishment over-achiever at a time of profound social and intellectual change – that some of the keys to Blacking's distinctive personality can be perceived: his complex and ambivalent attitudes towards authority and social radicalism, his profound sense of mission, his irrepressible energy.

To reflect on Blacking now is also to reflect on the completion of a number of posthumous projects, many of them aided by technological developments that became widespread very shortly after his death. He would surely have been delighted by the results. Reg Byron's edited series of key theoretical papers clarifies the broad development and consistency of this thought.[4] John Baily's careful restoration of his Venda films, and his ongoing published work on projects originally conceived and conducted with Blacking on instrument morphology, human movement and music structure, allow insights into Blacking's arguments about the embodied nature of musical experience, and an opportunity to put sound and physical movement together.[5] The restoration of the films has, of course, been crucial for those many of us who read Blacking's arguments, studied his detailed transcriptions, pored over the photographs and diagrams, but never had a chance to listen to the music or observe dancing and performing Venda bodies in motion. Suzel Reily and Lev Weinstock's recent CD-ROM/website goes a step further in making available to the public early recordings, transcriptions, film and detailed ethnography relating to his Venda girls initiation ceremony research – an invaluable resource.[6] Blacking's earliest published work often had the appearance of a website page. In *Venda Children's Songs* (1967), for example, the reader is directed hither and thither to diagrams, pictures, transcriptions, photos and sometimes two concurrent footnoting systems. It is a difficult book to read from cover to cover. The hypertext and multimedia possibilities of the Web are peculiarly appropriate to Blacking's way of thinking and explaining, and he would surely have availed himself of it had he lived long enough.

To reflect on Blacking now is also to celebrate success, both institutional and intellectual, at many different levels. His students and former colleagues lead ethnomusicological research in Europe, Africa, Australia and North America. A graduate degree in ethnomusicology from Queen's continues to guarantee disciplinary recognition and scholarly attention. The European Seminar in Ethnomusicology, founded by Blacking in 1981 specifically to keep those of us in Western Europe in touch with Eastern European colleagues and their incomparably rich traditions of music study, survived the traumas of the late 1980s and remains vibrant. The Society for Ethnomusicology, the American professional organisation, of which Blacking was once the only non-North American president, is now so prominent in intellectual life in the USA that it attracts tirades from right-wing opponents of political correctness on campus. The anthropological methods Blacking insisted on as ideals in ethnomusicological research – fluency in the languages and semiotic systems of a culture not one's own; extended fieldwork immersion; the ability to survey an entire social and cultural space when formulating theses and drawing conclusions – all now constitute norms in the discipline. It was not always so. Though his own habits of thought resisted complacency, it is hard not to come to the conclusion that had Blacking been alive today, he would have felt many of his goals, in putting ethnomusicology onto a productively institutionalised and professionalised footing, have been realised.

However, to reflect on Blacking in the early 2000s is also to enter polemicised waters, in which the history of ethnomusicology in Africa, and Blacking's contribution to it, finds itself under the microscope. There are two somewhat contradictory dynamics at play. One might be characterised as a defensive attitude to ethnomusicology in institutions committed to an elite and western view of music and music study. The other emanates from post-colonial theory, and the influential work of Edward Said, Homi Bhabha and Gayatri Spivak. Princeton music theorist Kofi Agawu's recent book, *Representing African Music*, is situated squarely in the somewhat contradictory space where these two currents converge.[7] The book reprises themes that have constituted a more or less continuous line of critique within anthropology, cultural study and literary criticism over two decades or so. This is that the representation of others in Western culture bears the marks of colonial encounter, that cultural difference is constructed in this encounter, that related claims to objectivity must be dismissed, and that ethnographic writing must both be read and produced against the grain if it is to yield any insights into real social, political and historical conditions.[8]

The primary focus of Agawu's criticism is the pursuit of difference in ethnomusicology. This, he argues, produces a distorted knowledge of African musical practices, as ethnomusicologists labour to interpret phenomena that might otherwise be straightforwardly described and explained. Metrical and rhythmic issues absorb Agawu. He argues persuasively that these have been particularly prone to mystification in the pursuit of difference. Agawu's argument also involves questions about formalism and the role of theory. This is perhaps the most contentious and polemic aspect of his argument, one that shatters the rather tense silence that has prevailed, at least in North America, for over a decade between ethnomusicologists and music theorists.[9] In essence, Agawu feels that ethnomusicologists are so preoccupied by culture (and the 'horizon of difference') that they fail to account for real African musical worlds. This entails firstly, in his view, a woeful lack of documentation of and interest in mission hymn singing, military bands, Western jazz, pop and rock, and the apparatus of Western music pedagogy in so many African countries.[10]

Far more importantly, though, it also denies Africans the propensity for formal play and an abstracted pleasure in that play that is held to be the domain of Western concert music only. Whatever these propensities and pleasures are, and whatever their relationship is to those at play in the domain of Western concert music, Agawu is concerned with the fact that ethnomusicology has, in the pursuit of 'difference', systematically deemed them not to exist at all, and ruled out of court any method or technique that might draw attention to them and illuminate them. A tactical methodological assumption of sameness (that African music be understood as *music*, and not 'African music') stands to correct this colonial bias, and restore to African musicians the kinds of skills, pleasures and agencies deemed to be the property of their colonial and post-colonial masters only.

Agawu's attitude to Blacking is ambivalent. This ambivalence betrays an awkward kinship between the colonial ethnographer and the post-colonial critic. For, on the one hand, Agawu situates Blacking very firmly in the world of colonial ethnography. The Venda, Agawu feels, are collectivised in Blacking's writing, and rarely treated as creative individuals. Blacking, Agawu points out, generalises from Venda experience to make pronouncements about Africa in general, and to establish its cardinal difference from 'the West'. Agawu portrays Blacking as a close follower of Viennese comparative musicologist Erich von Hornbostel, particularly in regard to Hornbostel's dictum concerning African rhythm: 'we proceed from sound, they from movement',[11] a dictum Agawu finds responsible for the most egregious mystifications and misrepresentations of African music. Finally, according to Agawu, Blacking tends to reduce musical structure to social structure. As a consequence, he is impatient with those who would dwell too long on musical surfaces, since what is interesting for Blacking is located elsewhere. One can certainly read Blacking's early writing to find evidence to back up Agawu's characterisation, but one can find much to contradict it too.[12]

On the other hand, Agawu finds much to praise in Blacking's work. An important section of Agawu's book deals with *Venda Children's Songs* (1967), a book Blacking – at the end of his life – considered, interestingly, to be undervalued by the ethnomusicological community. Blacking's fieldworking experimentalism interests Agawu, especially his technique of asking Venda children to clap the beats to their songs. An innocuous exercise, one might think, but, as Blacking explains, Venda children do not clap whilst they are singing, and found the exercise surprisingly complex, odd and counter-intuitive. The clapping patterns that he elicited reveal a rather more complex apprehension of rhythm and metre than one might at first suppose, a playful juggling of melodic stress, metrical accent and words. This Blacking relates, as he does many aspects of children's musical repertoire, to key structural features of the adult genre. One of the nostrums of a certain kind of culturalist ethnography, the kind that repels Agawu, is the assumption that 'native' texts are methodologically inviolable, particularly at the moment at which they are being recorded or documented. Though this kind of culturalism dates from a slightly later period than the research and writing of *Venda Children's Songs*, it is clear that, throughout his career, Blacking never had much time for this kind of thing. If a fieldworking ethnographer can defamiliarise familiar musical genres in the field to his informants, in the spirit of playful, collaborative experimentalism, Blacking felt, important insights might be gained.

Secondly, Agawu is interested in Blacking's habits of citing contemporary Western music theory. Blacking was inspired by the influential work of Viennese music theorist Hans Keller, who proposed, in the 1950s, a system of demonstrating the workings of the Austro-German art music tradition in and through music. He sought to avoid, or at least minimise, what he felt were the inevitable deformations that take place when non-linguistic sign systems are subordinated to the regimes of the written. The Venda *tshikona*, the national dance, fascinated Blacking, just as it fascinated the Venda. He described it, memorably, as a sonic waterfall, always moving, always staying in the same place, but also, he implied, as difficult to hold in one's hands – analytically speaking – as a waterfall. But in *Venda Children's Songs*, Blacking felt he could begin to explain, in

Keller's sense, 'the music behind the music', and thus to elucidate the rhythmic, modal and harmonic principles of the *tshikona* from within the Venda musical universe. This was not to say that Venda children's songs were simpler versions of something more complex. In some regards, he suggested, they were even more complex. But they were smaller in scale, more intimate, more conducive to slow-motion replay and the kind of playful, insight-generating fieldwork experimentation mentioned above.

Agawu is keen to note the 'professional alliance with the more mainstream analyst' Keller.[13] Agawu's comment is partly a suggestion that the sub-disciplinary antagonisms that have sometimes characterised the relations between music theorists and ethnomusicologists in the USA are a recent development, underpinned by a more sustained history of dialogue and conversation. I would agree with this characterisation, and Agawu's take on it. Disciplinary consolidation in ethnomusicology has, perhaps inevitably, resulted in graduate students and young professionals lacking familiarity with the traditions of Western music theory, and this is clearly problematic. But Agawu's characterisation also establishes a hierarchy: Blacking the ethnomusicologist is 'less mainstream', Keller the music theorist 'more mainstream'. This is harder to sustain. I think it is very hard to say what did and did not characterise 'mainstream' music study in the 1960s, just as it is now. I was, for example, strongly encouraged to read Blacking's *How Musical is Man?* as an undergraduate at the (extremely conservative) music department at Oxford in the early 1980s. I received no such encouragement to read Keller. In the wake of the so-called 'new musicology' of the last ten years or so, it is perhaps even more difficult to say what now constitutes 'mainstream' music study.[14]

Agawu is clearly nostalgic for a moment, supposedly represented by Blacking, in which ethnomusicologists knew their place. I don't think Blacking ever knew his place. His habits of citation were less strategic interventions in discussions between music theorists and ethnomusicologists, and more a reflection of energetic, uninhibited reading practices. Everything Blacking read was, one way or another, grist to his mill, and he read extremely widely. He would have found much to agree with in the post-colonial dimensions of Agawu's critique. Where it is complicit with colonial power, where it reproduces colonial fantasies of otherness and difference, where it advocates methodological apartheid ('one musicology for them, another for us'), ethnomusicologists are profoundly at fault. I believe there is much in Blacking's writing which advocates all of these points very forcefully, sometimes implicitly, and sometimes, as in his later writing, explicitly.

Like Agawu, Blacking also argued vociferously against accounts of music that simply show it reproducing the politically dominant social processes and cultural schemes. Blacking distinguished music – a deeply embodied proclivity to formal play that was capable, he felt, of patterning our relations with others – from 'music', socially sanctioned and historically specific instantiations of this capacity, however imperfectly or partially realised. It was of the essence of his account that our musical habits could disrupt our 'musical' habits, and that this disruption could have profound social and political consequences. Oppressed and disadvantaged people, he argued, with reference to the South African black churches, could feel the way they wanted to be in music long before they could devise coherent political strategies and arguments. If Agawu's 'strategic formalism' is about grasping music as a means of 'playing with signs',[15] if it means grasping music as a current of formalised energy and play that can never be fully accounted for by the dominant systems of interpretation and explanation (especially those provided by colonialism), I sense a profound and unacknowledged kinship with Blacking's central argument. Agawu, like Blacking, is interested in music rather than 'music'. Agawu, like Blacking, believes that culturally dominant means of explaining music can obscure rather than explain. Like Blacking he believes that small strategic interpretative deformations of the cultural fabric can provide the necessary critical angle and space. Unlike Blacking, Agawu feels that ethnomusicology's sub-disciplinary baggage renders it incapable of these moves. Blacking, I believe, demonstrates that Agawu is wrong.

My own efforts to suggest certain areas of common ground between Blacking and his most recent critics have two motivations, which I will mention briefly before closing. One is to agree with these critics in their characterisation of colonial era ethnomusicology, though to exempt Blacking from their stronger claims. Where ethnomusicology loses sight of its complex and thorny historical complicity with colonialism, it reproduces its myths. I don't believe Blacking was ever in danger of doing this, as an enduring consequence of his experiences in apartheid South Africa. The other is to question the kinds of hierarchy Agawu's critique implies between music theorists on the one hand, monopolising a superior kind of 'theoretical' discussion, and ethnomusicologists on the other, essentially confined to the role of diversity officers in music departments, making sure Western music theory doesn't forget others on the margins or over the horizon. Blacking's writings suggest a significantly more nuanced view of the relationship between ethnomusicology and music theory (and, indeed, the other musicological subdisciplines). In other regards, too, they continue to have much to teach us. His ethnomusicology embraced all: 'music' as it is and had been, music as it could be. It was rooted in a profound sense of the wholeness of social and cultural life and a profound sense of political possibility, two items in extremely short supply these days. Blacking was a Queen's thinker of singular distinction and influence. It is very appropriate for us to treasure his memory today.

[1] John Blacking, *Venda Children's Songs* (Johannesburg: Witwatersrand University Press, 1967); John Blacking, *How Musical Is Man?* (London: Faber & Faber, 1973); John Blacking, ed., *The Anthropology of the Body* (London: Academic Press, 1977); John Blacking, *A Common Sense View of All Music* (Cambridge: Cambridge University Press, 1987).

[2] See, for example, John Baily, 'John Blacking and his Place in Ethnomusicology', *Yearbook for Traditional Music* 22 (1990): xii–xxi; John Baily, 'John Blacking: Dialogue with the Ancestors' (John Blacking Memorial Lecture, London, Goldsmiths College, 1991); Keith Howard, 'John Blacking: An Interview Conducted and Edited by Keith Howard', *Ethnomusicology* 35, no. 1 (1991): 55–76. The 16th Annual Conference of the European Seminar in Ethnomusicology was held at Queen's University Belfast on 7–10 September 2000, a conference devoted to reflection on the work of John Blacking, attended by a large number of his former colleagues and students; the European Seminar in Ethnomusicology features a Blacking Memorial Lecture, given in recent years by Jeremy Montagu, Roderyk Lange, Anna Czekanowska, Jan Ling, John Baily, Gerhart Kubik and many others.

[3] Blacking was terminally ill when I arrived in Belfast from Oxford in November 1989.

4 Reginald Byron, *Music, Culture and Experience: Selected Papers of John Blacking* (Chicago: University of Chicago Press, 1995).
5 John Baily, 'Music and the Body', *The World of Music* 37, no. 2 (1995): 11–30.
6 Suzel Reily and Lev Weinstock, eds, *Venda Girls' Initiation Schools, by John Blacking* (CD-ROM; Belfast: Department of Anthropology, Queen's University Belfast, 1998).
7 Kofi Agawu, *Representing African Music: Postcolonial Notes, Queries, Positions* (New York: Routledge, 2003). For a related critique see also Martin Scherzinger, 'Negotiating the Music-theory/African-music Nexus: A Political Critique of Ethnomusicological Anti-Formalism and a Strategic Analysis of the Harmonic Patterning of the Shona Mbira Song Nyamaropa', *Perspectives of New Music* 39 (2001): 5–118.
8 The anthropological genealogy includes Talal Asad, ed., 1973, *Anthropology and the Colonial Encounter* (New York: Humanities Press, 1973); and James Clifford and George Marcus, eds, *Writing Culture: The Poetics and Politics of Ethnography* (Berkeley: University of California Press, 1986).
9 The term 'music theory', in North America, describes the musicological discipline most concerned with the analysis of musical works in the Western concert ('art') music canon, from Bach to Beethoven and beyond. Many, if not most, working in this tradition take their orientations from Heinrich Schenker (1868–1935), though his intellectual legacy is contested.
10 The extensive work of David Coplan, Veit Erlmann, Christopher Waterman, Carol Ann Muller, Paul Richards, John Collins and a great many others on exactly these kinds of musical traditions is, curiously, acknowledged by Agawu.
11 Erich von Hornbostel, 'On Negro Music', *Africa* 1, no. 1 (1928): 30–62.
12 The exhaustive transcriptions published in his early Venda initiation schools ethnography alone would seem to refute the charge that Blacking was uninterested in 'surface' musical detail (see Reily and Weinstock, *Venda Girls' Initiation Schools*).
13 Kofi Agawu, 'Review Article: John Blacking and the Study of African Music', *Africa* 67, no. 3 (1997): 99.
14 The following two titles might be taken as useful guides to generic and theoretical orientations of the 'new musicology' of the later 1980s and 1990s: Richard Leppert and Susan McClary, *Music and Society: The Politics of Composition, Performance and Reception* (Cambridge: Cambridge University Press, 1987); and Georgina Born and David Hesmondhalgh, *Western Music and its Others: Difference, Representation and Appropriation in Music* (California: University of California Press, 2000).
15 Phrase borrowed from the title of another of Kofi Agawu's influential books, *Playing With Signs* (Princeton: Princeton University Press, 1991).

Chronicling a University

Queen's, Belfast,
1945–2004

LESLIE CLARKSON

LESLIE CLARKSON is Emeritus Professor of Social History at Queen's University.

There are, broadly, three approaches to writing the history of a university. One is to concentrate on structures, benefactors, presidents and vice-chancellors. A second is to focus on the work of the scholars and students who make up the university. This is not an easy task because the scholarship of modern universities covers such a vast range of intellectual activity that is beyond the ability of a single author, or even several authors, to encompass.[1] A third approach is to recognise that universities are part of society and that their history is shaped by the values of that society.

Institutional changes are the easiest to deal with and they provide a framework for a fuller understanding of the university. Charters and statutes, major reorganisations, mergers or closures, offer a convenient chronology, while presidents and vice-chancellors become the *deus* (or *dei*) *ex machina* of all that is successful. Any misfortunes along the way can be ascribed to extraneous circumstances.

The limitation of concentrating on structures and the personalities at the top is that it simplifies the story. Take vice-chancellors, for example. When Eric Ashby, one of the most influential of all UK vice-chancellors, arrived at Queen's at the beginning of 1951, a retired professor told him his presence was as superfluous as the fifth wheel on a carriage, but that he was welcome nevertheless. The greeting was elegant but it missed the point. Vice-chancellors are necessary to steer the carriages through the tangled thickets of government policy and along paths pitted by potholes of inadequate funding. But they cannot do the job by themselves; they need good colleagues to help them along the way. Ashby understated his own role by remarking that if a vice-chancellor appoints the right staff all he has to do is to go around being nice to people. He was correct, however, in appreciating the limits on the powers of the office.[2]

The strengths of the institutional approach, nevertheless, are considerable and are demonstrated in the magisterial two-volume history of Queen's during its first one hundred years by T.W. Moody and J.C. Beckett.[3] Belfast was one of three colleges comprising the Queen's University in Ireland, established in 1845 (the other two were in Cork and Galway). The University of Dublin, now more commonly known as Trinity College Dublin, had been founded in 1592 for the education of Anglicans, and despite some opening of the college to non-Anglicans, by the early nineteenth century there was a pressing need for a system of higher education in Ireland acceptable to Catholics and Protestants alike.

The first volume of Moody and Beckett examines the debates in the Westminster parliament during 1844 and 1845 that led to the setting up of the Queen's colleges, the search for a suitable location in Belfast, the construction between 1845 and 1849 of what became known as the Lanyon Building, the appointment of the first professors, the designing of a curriculum, and the work of the first two presidents, the Reverend Pooley Shuldham Henry and the Reverend Josias Leslie Porter. The story continues through to the reorganisation of the Queen's University into the Royal University in 1879–80, and to the eventual independence of the northern college as the Queen's University of Belfast in 1908–9.

The second volume considers Queen's during its early years of independence, the difficulties caused by the First World War and the formation of the state of Northern Ireland, and the performance of the university during the financially constricted interwar years and the Second World War. It concludes in 1949. The year marked the anniversary of the first century of teaching. It also saw the departure of the fourth vice-chancellor, Sir David Keir, and the appointment of Eric Ashby as his successor. By now Queen's was a small university of dedicated staff serving the needs of a somewhat inward-looking region. Over the next half-century Queen's and Northern Ireland both experienced changes more momentous than anything that had occurred since partition.

The original Queen's University in Ireland, the Royal University that succeeded it, and the independent Queen's Belfast, were responses to the political and social circumstances of the time. As Moody and Beckett remark, the history of Queen's, 'from one point of view ... forms part of the history of government policy during the period of the union'.[4] None of the colleges imposed religious tests and all were open to all denominations, though Belfast's was Protestant in ethos and its first three presidents were all Presbyterian ministers. When the Belfast college gained its independence in

1908–9 it continued to reflect the religious and political beliefs held by the majority of the population in what eventually became the state of Northern Ireland.

The curriculum of the Queen's colleges evolved along lines similar to those in the new universities then being established in England. Until the second quarter of the nineteenth century Oxford and Cambridge offered an education mainly to the landed elite based on a study of the classics and mathematics. However, the universities founded after 1828, such as London, Durham, Owens College, Manchester and Birmingham, developed vocational courses, although the liberal philosophy of education for its own sake articulated by John Henry Newman in his Dublin lectures in 1852, and later published as *The Idea of a University*, continued to be highly influential.[5]

Queen's College Belfast had three faculties: arts, with two divisions (humanities and sciences), and the professional faculties of medicine and law. Medicine remained the largest professional school until the 1940s, with medical students accounting for one third of all students. The natural and applied sciences gained their own faculties in 1909, and eventually commerce (later economics and social sciences), agriculture and education became faculties in their own right. More recently, for reasons of 'managerial efficiency', the number of faculties has been reduced, first to five, then to three, although the range of subjects studied has increased greatly. Over the decades the humanities declined in relative importance, although the trend became pronounced only during the second half of the twentieth century. By the end of the century the traditional arts subjects – Latin and Greek – had all but expired, but there were new developments in areas such as anthropology, film and theatre studies, and music.

The Moody and Beckett volumes were written to commemorate the first one hundred years of Queen's. To mark its one hundred and fiftieth birthday the university published *Degrees of Excellence*, by Brian Walker and Alf McCreary.[6] It was a very different work from its predecessor, written in a relaxed style and lavishly illustrated. It was intended, in the words of the vice-chancellor at the time, Sir Gordon Beveridge, to be 'the people's history', popular and accessible.[7] Like their predecessors, the authors follow a chronological path, but the chapter headings – 'Changing Times', 'Hurricanes of Change', 'The Old Older Changeth', and so on – suggest not only a lighter touch but a greater emphasis on external influences. Within the chapters there is less focus on structures and governance than in Moody and Beckett. Student sporting and social activities figure prominently, perhaps more prominently than students' academic achievements. Discussion of the scholarly work of the university is confined, as it was in Moody and Beckett, to noting the presence of a few outstanding scholars.

As well as commissioning *Degrees of Excellence*, the vice-chancellor invited the present author to write a history of the university during the second half of the twentieth century. Changing public perceptions of what universities should be doing suggested that this study should focus heavily on the relationship between Queen's and the wider community. Queen's Belfast, and its antecedents had all been creations of the government. But beyond drawing the sting of sectarian rivalry from the problem of higher education in Ireland, what did the government want them to do?

During the nineteenth and the first half of the twentieth century there had been plenty of discussion in Britain and Ireland among educational philosophers about the functions of universities, but less in government circles and little that added up to a coherent policy. This changed in 1963 with the publication of the Robbins Report.[8] One commentator remarked, with some exaggeration, that until Robbins 'because universities were autonomous the main policy of government towards higher education should be to have no policy'.[9] Even before the Robbins Committee met it was clear that universities had a part to play in national life. The Second World War had demonstrated their importance in developing technologies essential to the successful prosecution of the conflict and, in the longer term, in contributing to post-war economic regeneration. In 1952 Queen's argued for an increase in government funding because 'skilled and enlightened citizens, essential for this country's struggle for national recovery, are not being produced in sufficient quantity'.[10] There was now a lively debate about how universities could combine the liberal tradition of scholarship with the need for technological education. A leading participant in the debate was Eric Ashby, whose *Technology and the Academics* was published in 1958, when he was vice-chancellor of Queen's.[11]

The Robbins Committee identified four interlocking purposes of higher education: the cultivation of skills, the development of the mind, the advancement of learning, and the transmission of a 'common culture and common standards of citizenship'. There was a strong echo of Newman in these aims. When the Lockwood Committee published its report on higher education in Northern Ireland two years later, it largely accepted the premises set out by Robbins.[12] Both reports inaugurated a period of expansion in higher education, including new universities in Britain and Northern Ireland (the New University of Ulster), financed mainly by taxpayers.

Queen's shared in the expansion. Immediately after the war it had a student population of nearly two and a half thousand. Half a century later there were more than sixteen thousand students at the university, excluding those in the teacher-training colleges (now university colleges) and the Institute of Lifelong Learning. Numbers rose in the later 1940s as ex-servicemen and -women, including a considerable number from Britain, entered to resume their studies. Thereafter the figures remained more or less static until the mid-1950s. Two-thirds of students – or their parents – paid their own fees and fewer than 4 per cent of 17–20 year olds went to university, in Queen's or elsewhere. There was a sustained increase in numbers during the 1960s. The educational reforms contained in the Butler Act of 1944, which became law in Northern Ireland in 1947, opened up the possibility of higher education to all children regardless of social class; the effects began to feed through to Queen's by the early 1960s. More importantly, mandatory grants for university entrants, paid by the local authorities, were introduced in 1961–2. According to the vice-chancellor, Dr Michael Grant, grants resulted in weak students 'flocking to Queen's'. Even so, university education remained socially skewed, and as late as 1973 three-quarters of Northern Ireland undergraduates came from non-manual backgrounds.

Growth slackened during the 1970s. The New University of Ulster, established in 1965, was now taking students, and the post-Robbins universities in Britain also attracted undergraduates from Northern Ireland, particularly from middle-class Protestant families, as the Troubles bit into everyday life. During the worst of the

Troubles in the early 1970s, the numbers of students leaving Northern Ireland to go to universities or polytechnics in Britain accounted for over 40 per cent of all Northern Ireland's entrants into higher education. Student numbers in Queen's rose again from the late 1970s, with a temporary stutter at the end of the twentieth century, possibly caused by the re-introduction of student fees. By now the proportion of the relevant age cohort entering higher education was hovering at around 40 percent.

Throughout the 1960s and early 1970s governments (and taxpayers) were generally willing to meet the rising costs of higher education. But doubts grew during the 1970s, provoked in part by the student unrest at the end of the 1960s, but more directly by inflation and a perceived need to curb the growth in public expenditure. In Northern Ireland, university funding came from the Stormont government, advised by the University Grants Committee (UGC). In the late 1940s Queen's had limped along on an annual income of a quarter of a million pounds and was the poorest university in the United Kingdom by a considerable margin. At the end of the century its annual income exceeded £226 million (the equivalent of £6 million in 1940s values), the bulk of it from central or local taxation. Spending per student in the 1980s was five times greater in real terms than in the 1940s, although it fell back by nearly 20 per cent over the next decade. There were good reasons for the increase, including bringing the standards of student facilities closer to the levels enjoyed in British universities, and the growing costs of research.

The increased participation in university education was generally welcomed in Northern Ireland, particularly as it was accompanied by a larger proportion of women among the student population in Queen's, rising from around 20–25 per cent of the total in the 1950s to more than 50 per cent by the end of the century. The numbers of Catholic students attending Queen's also increased significantly. During the inter-war years they accounted for around 20 per cent of the total; and in the early 1960s Catholics still made up only a quarter of students at Queen's, well below their share of the Northern Ireland population. The proportion then grew steadily until at the end of the twentieth century 54 per cent of Queen's students were Catholics, a higher percentage than the proportion aged 18–24 in the population of Northern Ireland (48 per cent in

1991).[13] This increase has been attributed in part to the fact that Catholics from less well-off backgrounds were more likely to engage in higher education than Protestants from similar backgrounds. Catholic students from manual backgrounds saw higher education as a means of improving their socio-economic status. Protestant university entrants continued to be mainly middle-class, and many of them opted to study at universities in England or Scotland, whereas for Catholic students Queen's was the first choice.

The rising proportion of Catholics among Queen's students would have been unremarkable but for the fact that it accompanied, and was part of, the political upheavals that engulfed Northern Ireland in the late 1960s. Queen's was unique among UK universities in that it was located in a community where a substantial minority of the population disputed the legitimacy of the state and felt that it discriminated against them.[14] Events surrounding the civil rights marches of the late 1960s escalated into three decades of violence. Queen's was caught in the fallout. Some of the students joined their political beliefs to youthful radicalism – at its height in the late 1960s – and for several years student politics were conducted on nationalist–unionist lines.

Some of the Catholic student-radicals – as well as some politicians outside – demanded that Queen's should align itself in the struggle against what they perceived to be an unjust society. Queen's refused to become involved in the political turmoil, agreeing in 1974 with its chancellor (Lord Ashby, the former vice-chancellor) that 'universities that have corporately dabbled in politics have lost their influence and liberties'.[15] In 1977, when the political turmoil was at its height, Sir Peter Froggatt, the vice-chancellor, pointed out that universities have traditionally been custodians of the values of societies and not the agents of change. If Queen's were to adopt a particular position in the current political turmoil it would enrage large sections of the community because there was no generally agreed correct position.[16]

Although Queen's tried to stand above the Troubles, its buildings were damaged by bombs and bullets. Several students and two members of staff were murdered, and there were difficulties in recruiting and retaining good staff. Its reputation in some sections of the wider community suffered from a perception that Queen's or the Students' Union (the critics did not always make a distinction) were getting too close to nationalist and republican views.

The public image of Queen's was badly damaged at the end of the 1980s by allegations that it had been and was continuing to discriminate against Catholics when making staff appointments. For five years its reputation was battered by adverse publicity. In a gesture of goodwill to the nationalist community Queen's decided no longer to play the UK national anthem at graduation ceremonies. The decision caused uproar among the unionist community, of an intensity bewildering to anybody outside Northern Ireland. Queen's was adjusting painfully to major changes in the social structure of Northern Ireland and was caught in the classic dilemma: the more it tried to accommodate one side the more it alienated the other.[17]

Amidst the political brouhaha surrounding Queen's, it is easy to forget that it was subjected to the financial pressures experienced by all UK universities during the 1980s and 1990s. The Westminster government – with Stormont in its wake – reduced the per capita expenditure on higher education and queried whether universities had been providing good value for money. In order to reassure itself – though not the academics – and the public at large that financial constraints were not lowering standards, the government introduced procedures to measure the quality of teaching and research in universities. Teaching and research audits pushed the affairs of universities further into the public arena.

Queen's had always prided itself on high standards of teaching and research, but until the 1980s the evidence on both was patchy and impressionistic. The arts degree had been reformed in 1955 because, it was widely accepted within the university, it was not nurturing intellectual maturity sufficiently, and high failure rates in one or two subjects suggested that something was amiss.[18] Students had had no formal mechanisms for commenting on the quality of teaching. A short-lived experiment with a staff–student committee in the medical faculty in 1944, which produced some useful modifications in examination procedures, failed to spread to other faculties. Students gradually became more vocal, however. The Students' Representative Council carried out a survey of student opinion in 1968 that revealed mixed feelings about the quality of lectures and staff–student committees were introduced in 1972. In 1994 a survey of graduating students revealed a high level of satisfaction with the quality of lectures but considerably less with tutorials, seminars and practical classes.

The first externally directed teaching audits were held in 1990. Queen's emerged from successive exercises firmly established among the top quartile of UK universities for teaching. It remained an open question, however, whether the criteria used really were measures of good teaching – teaching that stimulates intellectual excitement – or whether they were measures of student satisfaction, which is not quite the same thing.

Even so, Queen's could be pleased that it stood high in teaching league tables. When it came to research the picture was less comforting. In 1955 the secretary to the Academic Council described research as 'organised curiosity', a description that captured the almost gentlemanly attitude to research at the time.[19] Scholars such as Michael Roberts and Lewis Warren (history), Kenneth Connell (economic history), E. Estyn Evans (geography), Martin Jope (archaeology), David Bates and Alex Dalgarno (theoretical physics), Bernard Crossland (engineering), Alwyn Williams (geology), R.D.C. Black (economics) and John Blacking (anthropology) produced scholarship that would have graced any university. Every year the vice-chancellor's reports recorded a substantial volume of published work, and from 1967 the university's accounts reported rising income received from research councils and contracts. Queen's was well satisfied with its performance.

In 1986 the UGC conducted the first national assessment of the quality of research in universities throughout the United Kingdom. Research areas were graded as 'below average', 'average', 'above average', or 'excellent'. It came as a shock to Queen's when only social anthropology was rated as excellent and more than half its subjects as below average. The university found itself reading depressing headlines in the local press proclaiming its poor research record.

In subsequent years the assessment methods were refined according to a numerical scale, with 5* and 5 indicating internationally excellent research, 4 and 3, mixes of international and national excellence, and 2 and 1 suggesting that the research achievements were of little scholarly significance. In 1989 Queen's was again judged to have an unhealthy proportion of undistinguished research, with 30 out of 49 research areas rated as 1 or 2. There were substantial improvements over the next decade. What became known as the Research Assessment Exercise (RAE) made it possible to compare research in Queen's with that in other UK universities. Queen's began to emerge respectably from the comparison, though not in the top league.

Many academics were sceptical about the assessment processes, arguing that they measured the quantity of research, not its quality. This, though, was a debate within universities. As far as the general population in Northern Ireland was concerned league tables of research seemed to add to their knowledge about Queen's and make comparisons possible with the local rival, the University of Ulster. The research grades at Queen's were generally higher than those of its neighbour, but the comparison did not necessarily work in Queen's favour since there was a public perception that the University of Ulster was doing research more immediately directed to the needs of the community.

Since 1945 Queen's has adapted itself to changing social and political circumstances. It has grown in size – initially with a good deal of reluctance – as government education strategies resulted in increased numbers of school leavers entering higher education. As a result a larger proportion of the Northern Ireland population came to have direct knowledge of Queen's. As mentioned above, its teaching and research became subject to external evaluation, and the ways the university set about these tasks were adapted accordingly. In teaching, great attention is now paid to 'student feedback' on the quality of the instruction they receive. Research has ceased to be an activity followed by individuals or groups of individuals as the fancy took them, but is coordinated by a university research committee so as to attract grants from the research councils and achieve the highest grades from the external assessors.

Even the language employed by the university to describe its activities has been modified over the years so as to give it a more burnished image. In 1908 Queen's described its task as that of spreading 'learning throughout the land', the land in question being that of the then undivided Ireland. At the beginning of the twenty-first century such modest tones would no longer serve. Now the university has a mission statement declaring that it is working in a 'global academic environment'.[20]

Some of the changes experienced by Queen's have been the consequences of local circumstances. For instance, the growing number of Catholic students reflected the changing position of Catholics in Northern Ireland society. The proportion of Catholics among the staff, particularly among the non-academic grades, increased as Queen's scrupulously observed fair employment legislation that governs all employers in Northern Ireland. In this, as in other matters, Queen's was adapting to shifts in society. This is not to say that the university was without influence in shaping the wider social and political changes. Queen's was, after all the principal source of professional men and women in Northern Ireland; their actions and ideas fed into the heady brew that was public opinion in the region. The great majority of Queen's students and a large proportion of its staff were born and bred in Northern Ireland and they shared the views, concerns and fears of their fellow citizens. But no one could seriously claim that Queen's was in the van of the convulsions that shook society for three decades from the 1960s.

The task of the historian is to interpret the past, and those interpretations reflect contemporary concerns. In the second half of the twentieth century the affairs of all universities became subject to public scrutiny to a greater degree than at any time during the previous century. Within Northern Ireland there was the added dimension of political upheaval colouring the ways in which the university was regarded by the world beyond its walls. It is worth reflecting, in conclusion therefore, on which had the greater impact: the forces affecting all UK universities, or those that were peculiar to Northern Ireland.

Between 1950 and the early twentieth century, Queen's, in line with all universities, grew in size; females formed a greater proportion of the student population, especially in disciplines such as the natural sciences and engineering; and – to a lesser extent – undergraduates were drawn from a wider social background. These developments were the consequences of the desire of successive governments to raise the proportion of school leavers entering higher education. This, in addition to the influence of the Robbins report, led to an increase in the number of universities in the UK while in Northern

Ireland, post-1965, Queen's was having to share the local stage with the New University of Ulster.[21]

With the expansion of the sector, the mission of universities changed. No longer could they be, if they ever had been, purely Newmanite temples for the training of the mind. Queen's had traditionally balanced liberal and vocational education; and it maintained its commitment to liberal studies in the second half of the twentieth century, notwithstanding the increase of vocational courses.

The most important national development began in the early 1980s when universities began to suffer sustained per capita reductions in funding based on student numbers. Because of the peculiar financial arrangements between Westminster and Stormont the cuts were felt especially severely in Northern Ireland. The University Grants Committee, which since 1919 had acted as a buffer between the government and the universities, was replaced by bodies that took a more interventionist approach in the way money was spent.[22] The result was that universities were forced to look to industry and the research councils for more of their income and vice-chancellors became managers who shaped the framework within which research was conducted. The government-inspired RAE and teaching quality assessments changed the university scholar from a self-motivated individual into one whose professional life was regulated by research and teaching targets set from the centre. It was an experience shared to various degrees by everybody working in publicly funded bodies.

Since the 1960s Northern Ireland's political and social landscapes have changed and all institutions – central and local government, the police, the civil service, private employers, schools and hospitals – have had to respond to the changing circumstances. Queen's, because of its long association with that part of Ireland that eventually became Northern Ireland, was identified with the old order. The pressing task for the university was to demonstrate that it was a place of learning open to all who were qualified to benefit from the education it offered, regardless of religious or political affiliation. Was this a greater challenge than that of having to adapt to growing size and difficult funding arrangements? There is no certain way of answering the question, although it is worth remembering the words of the Irish Universities Act, 1908, 'no test whatever of religious belief shall be imposed on any person' becoming or continuing as a member of the university.

At the beginning of the twenty-first century Northern Ireland is moving into a more peaceful political era and Queen's is able to give its full attention to its scholarly mission. The question has become how to balance its contribution to the world of scholarship with its responsibilities to the local community. Reputation and – crucially – funding depend on pursuing scholarship judged to be of international excellence. Can success on the international stage be achieved and maintained without compromising the university's duty to educate the highly qualified men and women that Northern Ireland needs? The future historian who attempts to chronicle the next fifty years of the history of Queen's might be in a better position to answer that question.

---

1   A brave attempt to embrace the whole range of scholarship is the recent history of the University of Nottingham by Brian Tolley, a monumental two-volume work of 1388 pages. Volume 2 serves as an academic *Who's Who* from the granting of the charter in 1948 to almost the end of the century. It is of interest principally to past and present members of the university. B.H. Tolley, *The History of the University of Nottingham*, 2 vols (Nottingham: Nottingham University Press, 2001).
2   For an assessment of Ashby, see Harold Silver, *Higher Education and Opinion Making in Twentieth-century England* (London and Portland, Oreg.: Woburn Press, 2003), 151–73. The professor who welcomed Ashby was H.O. Meredith, who occupied the chair of economics for more than thirty years as a somewhat detached member of the Bloomsbury Group. See S. Gourley Putt, 'A Packet of Bloomsbury Letters: The Forgotten H.O. Meredith', *Encounter* 59 (November, 1982): 77–84. Ashby made his remark to Alf McCreary, formerly Director of Information, Queen's University.
3   T.W. Moody and J.C. Beckett, *Queen's, Belfast, 1845–1949. The History of a University*, 2 vols (London: Faber & Faber, 1959).
4   Moody and Beckett, *Queen's, Belfast*, 2: 538.
5   R.D. Anderson, *Universities and Elites in Britain Since 1800* (Basingstoke: Macmillan, 1992), 12–16. In 1851 Newman had been invited by Archbishop Cullen of Armagh to advise on the Catholic University of Ireland being planned in Dublin and to 'give a few lectures on education'. Newman's concept of a liberal education did not preclude universities teaching

professional or vocational courses. See Ian Ker, *John Henry Newman: A Biography* (Oxford: Clarendon Press, 1988), 376, 390–2.

6   Brian Walker and Alf McCreary, *Degrees of Excellence: The Story of Queen's, Belfast, 1845–1995* (Belfast: Institute of Irish Studies, 1994).

7   The description was never made publicly, but was used several times in committee meetings.

8   *Higher Education: Report of the Committee Appointed by the Prime Minister under the Chairmanship of Lord Robbins, 1961–63* (report and five appendices, London, 1963).

9   Quoted in Silver, *Higher Education*, 184.

10 Quoted in L.A. Clarkson, *A University in Troubled Times: Queen's Belfast, 1945–2000* (Dublin: Four Courts Press, 2004), 27.

11 Ashby's thinking is discussed by Harold Silver in 'The Making of a Missionary: Eric Ashby and Technology', *History of Education* 31, no. 6 (2002): 557–70.

12 Clarkson, *A University in Troubled Times*, 6, 29–30; The Government of Northern Ireland, *Higher Education in Northern Ireland* (Belfast, 1965). The chairman was Sir John Lockwood, Master of Birkbeck College, London

13 R.D. Osborne, *Higher Education in Ireland North and South* (London: Jessica Kingsley, 1996), 34–7.

14 The University of Ulster (previously the New University of Ulster) was in a similar position, but it had been founded only in 1965 and did not carry the historical baggage of identification with the Union that burdened Queen's.

15 Quoted in Clarkson, *A University in Troubled Times*, 179.

16 Peter Froggatt, 'The University as an Instrument of Social Change: A Dangerous or a Desirable Concept?' (This was an address delivered to a meeting of representatives of Queen's and local schools in 1977. It was later published as a pamphlet by the Council of Queen's University and Schools, Belfast, 1977).

17 For a discussion see Clarkson, *A University in Troubled Times*, 175–91.

18 Clarkson, *A University in Troubled Times*, 151–2.

19 *Gown*, 12 May 1955.

20 'Queen's: Vision and Strategic Directions 2005–2015' (Belfast: Queen's University Belfast, 2005). This was a paper presented to Senate in 2005.

21 On the other hand, from the early 1960s the numbers of students from Northern Ireland going to Trinity College Dublin declined.

22 After partition the remit of the UGC did not extend to Northern Ireland but the Stormont administration normally sought and accepted its advice.

Afterword

PETER GREGSON
Current Vice-chancellor of Queen's University

Sir George Bain's Foreword eloquently and succinctly charts the context within which Queen's thinkers have shaped the past glories and the future destiny of this fine university. I concur with his analysis that no other university in the United Kingdom or Ireland has served and shaped its local community in the way Queen's has, while at the same time contributing to the global research community. The university remains at the forefront of thinking, but the context is changing at Queen's, in the local community, and in the wider environment.

The university's outlook was further expanded in November 2006 with its accession to the Russell Group of twenty leading UK universities. The Russell Group was formed in 1994 as an association of research-intensive universities, and is recognised around the globe. Queen's is the only university to have joined this grouping since its formation, and this historic development confirms Queen's standing as an international centre of academic excellence.

This volume reflects on the enormous contribution of the university's academics to society in Northern Ireland and beyond these shores. The period of history referred to as the Troubles left its impact on Queen's. At a time when others were looking outwards to the international community with increasing confidence, Queen's had to concentrate on providing a secure environment for academic scholarship in Northern Ireland. The past ten years have seen Queen's emerge increasingly strongly from this period of history, and Russell Group membership reflects the extraordinary talents of its staff and its students. Queen's now sits with pride alongside the other great civic universities of the United Kingdom and Ireland.

As this volume goes to print, members of the Northern Ireland

Assembly are assuming their new roles and responsibilities within the Assembly and Executive. Ministers, accountable to the people of Northern Ireland, once more have responsibility for shaping the future for the people. Queen's has a responsibility to work with those in elected office, and those who support them, to ensure that the contribution of higher education to the economic, social and cultural development of Northern Ireland is recognised. A new Northern Ireland is being built, with Queen's leading the development of a confident society ready to harness the creativity and the innovation of its people.

At the heart of this society is economic development, and Queen's is leading the way in the acquisition and exploitation of knowledge. World-class research centres with strong links to industry fuel the knowledge economy. Queen's University Ionic Liquids Laboratory (QUILL) is one example, and their pioneering work to develop pollution-free chemical processes was awarded a Queen's Anniversary Prize in 2006. Our Institute for Electronics, Communications and Information Technology (ECIT) is another.

One indicator of the university's contribution to society is its success in turning research ideas into wealth-creating businesses, and Queen's now tops the UK league tables with its spin-out companies contributing over £80m per annum of export sales to the Northern Ireland economy. This is a remarkable contribution to Northern Ireland, and it has to be seen alongside Queen's patronage of the arts and culture, its contribution to the development of public policy, and its role as a training ground for the professions.

Geographically, the university occupies a strategic position enjoying vital north-south, European and transatlantic linkages. In very specific ways, Queen's has been deepening its connections with the United States. In September 2006 Queen's signed a partnership agreement with Georgetown University in Washington DC, a university which shares many of the same challenges and opportunities. The Queen's–Georgetown Partnership embraces the Lombardi Cancer Centre in Georgetown and the Centre for Cancer Research and Cell Biology at Queen's – two world-leading research groups linked by the common desire to remain at the forefront of the development of innovative cancer treatments and new approaches to patient care.

Common interests in poetry resulted in prominent Queen's poets playing centre stage at both the Lannan Symposium in Georgetown and in a remarkable exposition of verse at the National Geographic in Washington in 2007 – a memorable highlight of the government's Rediscover Northern Ireland programme. Further common interests in post-conflict resolution and human rights will underpin the Mitchell Symposium in 2008, a flagship international conference celebrating the tenth anniversary of the signing of the Belfast Agreement and the role played by our chancellor, Senator George Mitchell. This symposium will enable scholars, politicians and practitioners from legal and community backgrounds to come together and debate the future challenges; it promises to be one of the highlights of a year of celebration marking the centenary of the granting of the University Charter.

As the business community has come together across the two jurisdictions on this island, so too the universities are working ever more closely together. This is especially the case for Queen's, University College Dublin and Trinity College Dublin, between them arguably the powerhouse of research on the island of Ireland. There have been extensive collaborations in the past: the Centre for Supercomputing in Ireland was the first large cross-border research collaboration. And now a partnership between Queen's and these two fine universities will have far-reaching consequences on future research and teaching programmes as, together, we seek to provide an academic experience which competes with the best in the world. In this context, pioneering proposals for research in the field of cystic fibrosis and diabetes are being submitted to the National Institutes of Health in the USA under the US–Ireland R&D Partnership Agreement.

In looking forward, Queen's links with the major scholarly societies across these islands assume a particular importance. The British Academy Symposium 'Who's Creating Knowledge?' and the Royal Academy of Engineering Exhibition and Soirée 'Wealth Creation Through Partnership' held at Queen's in 2007 demonstrate the university's ongoing connections with premier learned bodies. Events such as these provide a vital environment for the development of future generations of Queen's thinkers.

Acknowledgements

Queen's Thinkers owes much to the help the editors have received from various sources. Primarily we wish to acknowledge the support of the Queen's University's R.M. Jones Lecture Fund which sponsored the original conference where the following chapters were first presented, and the publication of the book itself. The skills of Una Reid in coordinating the conference are gratefully acknowledged as well as the willing participation of those who chaired the different sessions – Ken Bell, Margaret Mullett, John McCanny and Ellen Douglas-Cowie. The staff of Blackstaff Press have been a pleasure to work with and we are especially grateful to Patsy Horton and Michelle Griffin for their interest in and enthusiasm for this project. The Naughton Gallery of Queen's University also provided valuable assistance with the illustrations, as did Gill Alexander and Maura Pringle of the university's School of Geography, Archaeology and Palaeoecology. The following list indicates the sources and attributions of the figures.

ii	Photograph reproduced by kind permission of the Photographic Unit at Queen's University Belfast
1	Photograph reproduced by kind permission of the Photographic Unit at Queen's University Belfast
69	Photograph reproduced by kind permission of the Estate of Helen Waddell
83	Picture reproduced by kind permission of Balliol College, Oxford
93	Copyright holder not traced
105	Photograph © the University of Hull, reproduced with the kind permission of Hull University Archives
115	Eric Ashby by Ruskin Spear, reproduced by kind permission of the Bridgeman Art Library
131	E. Estyn Evans by W.F. Little; copyright holder not traced
141	David Bates by Basil Blackshaw, reproduced by kind permission of the artist
149	Copyright holder not traced
159	Copyright holder not traced
171	Photograph reproduced by kind permission of the Photographic Unit at Queen's University Belfast

ACKNOWLEDGEMENTS

Every effort has been made to trace and contact copyright holders before publication. If notified, the publisher will rectify any errors or omissions at the earliest opportunity.

Index

Abelard, Peter 74, 79
Aberdeen University vii, 13
Académie Royale de Belgique 147
Adams, Sir John 97
Agassiz, Louis 65
Agawu, Kofi 164–9
Alcuinus, Flaccus Albinus (Alcuin of York) 78–9
Alliance Party 147
American Academy of Arts and Sciences 147
Amis, Kingsley 108–9
Andrews, John 35–6
Andrews, Thomas 11, 13, 63
Annála Ríoghachta Éireann (*Annals of the Four Masters*) 37–8
Annals of the Four Masters 37–9; *see also Annála Ríoghachta Éireann* (*Annals of the Four Masters*)
Annan, Noel 125
A Paper Landscape 35
Arnold, Matthew 73–4
Arnott, Winifred 111
A Rumoured City: New Poets from Hull 109
Ashby, Eric (Lord Ashby of Brandon) ix, xi
  administrator 119–29
    management style 119–20, 122–3
  biographical details
    appearance *115*, 119
    death 127
    early life 118
    education
      City of London School 118
      learns German 118
      London Academy of Music 118
      Royal College of Science and Technology 118
    family 117
    health 127
    knighted 126
    marriage 118
    membership of societies, committees, etc. 128
      Advisory Council on Scientific and Industrial Research 125
      chairman, Carnegie Corporation-sponsored commission to advise on post-secondary education in Nigeria 126
      chairman, Northern Ireland Advisory Council for Education 125
      chairman, Postgraduate Grants Committee, Department of Scientific and Industrial Research 125
      chairman, Scientific Grants Committee, Department of Scientific and Industrial Research 125
      Inter-University Council 125
      Nuffield Provincial Hospitals Trust 125
      Tizard Advisory Council on Scientific Policy 125
      UK Committee of Vice-chancellors and Principals 125
      University Grants Committee 125
      vice-chairman, Association of Universities of the British Commonwealth 125
      vice-president, Council for Encouragement of Music and the Arts 125
    personality/character 119–20, 122, 127–8
    politics 179
    professional appointments
      assists in planning of Australian National University 117
      Clare College Cambridge 120
      Commonwealth Fund Fellowship (Chicago) 118
      Queen's University Belfast 117, 119–20, 173–4
      Royal College of Science and Technology (later Imperial College of Science and Technology, University of London) 118
      scientific counsellor and chargé d'affaires at Australian Legation, Moscow 117, 119

194 INDEX

University of Bristol 118
University of Manchester 117, 119
University of Sydney 117
public speaker 119, 125
raised to peerage 127
renown 125, 128
sport 120
violinist 118, 120
publications
   Environment and Plant Development
      (as translator) 118
   German–English Botanical
      Terminology 118
   Technology and the Academics 176
   The Rise of the Student Estate 125
research/ideas
   botany 117
   pedagogy 117–18, 120–3, 125–6,
      128
   translator 118
Ashby, Helen 117–18, 127
Ashby, Helena Maria 118
Ashby, Herbert Charles 118
Ashby, Michael 117, 120
Ashby, Peter 117
Aspect, Alain 101
Association of Universities of the British
   Commonwealth 125
Auden, W.H. 110, 112–13
Australian National University 117

Bacon, Francis 21–2
Baily, John 162
Bain, Sir George 187
Baldwin, James Mark 24, 26
Balliol College Oxford 73, 85–6, 89
Barrie, J.M. 13
Bates, Lady Barbara 147
Bates, Sir David xi
   biographical details
      appearance *141*
   education
      Queen's University Belfast 143,
         146
      University College London 143
   elected Fellow of Royal Society 147
   family 147
      Lady Barbara Bates 147
   friendships/collaborations
      Agnes Witherspoon 145
      Alexander Dalgarno 146–7

      Harrie Massey 143
      Lyman Spitzer 146
      Paul Hays 145
   knighted 147
   membership of academies
      Académie Royale de Belgique 147
      American Academy of Arts and
         Sciences 147
      Royal Irish Academy 147
      United States National Academy of
         Sciences 147
   nominated for Nobel Prize xi
   personality 147
   politics 147
      founding member of Alliance Party
         147
   professional appointments
      Queen's University Belfast 143–4
      University College London 143–4
   concern for the environment 145–6
   research/ideas
      aeronomy 143–4
      applied mathematics 143
      atmospheric science 145
      atomic physics 144–5
      dissociative recombination 143–4
      molecular physics 144–6
      optical physics 144–5
      physics of ionosphere 143
      quantum mechanics 144
Baudelaire, Charles 71, 73, 76
Beckett, J.C. xi, 135, 151
   biographical details
      appearance *149*
      early life 151
   education
      Queen's University Belfast 151–2
   elected to Royal Irish Academy 152
   friendships/collaborations
      D.B. Quinn 151
      R.B. McDowell 151
      R.E. Glasscock 154
      T.W. Moody 151–3
   politics 151–2, 155–7
   professional appointments
      Queen's University Belfast 152,
         157
   religiosity 155, 157
   retirement 152
   publications
      A Short History of Ireland 152, 154–6

Belfast: Origins and Growth of an Industrial City 154
Confrontations: Studies in Irish History 152
contributor to press 154
Irish Historical Studies (as contributor) 152–3
Protestant Dissent in Ireland, 1687–1780 152–3
Queen's Belfast, 1845–1949 3, 152–3, 173, 175–6
The Anglo-Irish Tradition 152, 154
The Cavalier Duke: A Life of James Butler, 1st Duke of Ormond 152
The Making of Modern Ireland 152, 154–5, 157
Ulster Since 1800: A Political and Economic Survey 154
radio contributor 153–5
research/ideas
  historiography 151–5, 157
    Anglo-Irish tradition 152, 154, 156–7
    autonomy of Irish history 156
    joint-founder of Irish Historical Society 153
    joint-founder of Studies in Irish History 153
    joint founder of Ulster Society for Irish Historical Studies 153
    'New History of Ireland' 153
    perspective 153–6
    source-based 152–4, 156–7
    teleology 153, 155
    'The Study of Irish History' lecture 155–6
  literature 154
Bédier, Joseph 75
Belfast Group (poetry) 112
Belfast Natural History and Philosophical Society 63
Belfast Social Inquiry Society 62
Belfast Technical High School 95
Bell (née Ross), Mary 96–7, 103
Bell, John Stewart xi
  biographical details
    appearance 93
    early life 95
    education
      Belfast Technical High School 95
      Fane Street Elementary School (Belfast) 95
      Queen's University Belfast 95, 98
      Ulsterville Avenue Elementary School (Belfast) 95
      University of Birmingham 96–8
    elected Fellow of Royal Society 103
    friendships/collaborations
      Franz Mandl 96, 98
      Jack Steinberger 98
      Jon Leinaas 97
      Martinus Veltman 98
      Mary Bell (née Ross) 96–7, 103
      Sir John Adams 97
    influences
      Robert Harvey Sloane 95, 98
      George Emeleus 95, 98
      Paul Ewald 95
    marriage 96
    personality 103
    professional appointments
      Atomic Energy Research Establishment (Harwell) 95–8
      European Centre for Nuclear Research (CERN) 96–8
      Queen's University Belfast 95
      Stanford Linear Accelerator Center 97
      University of Birmingham 96
    nominated for Nobel Prize 103
    publications
      paper, 'On the Einstein-Podolsky-Rosen Paradox' 100–1
      paper, *Reviews of Modern Physics* 98
      Selected Papers of John S. Bell (eds. M. Bell, K. Gottfried, M. Veltman) 98
    research/ideas
      accelerator physics 96–7
      CPT theorem 96, 98
        charge conjugation 96
        parity inversion 96
        time reversal 96
      elementary particle physics 96, 98
      locally realistic theory 100–1
      nuclear physics 98
      quantum theory 95–103
      reactor physics 95, 98
Benedictbeuern, Monastery of 75
Benson, Sir Frank 50
Betts, R.R. 85, 90
Beveridge, Sir Gordon 175
Bhabha, Homi 164
Bibliothèque Nationale (Paris) 75

INDEX

Black, R.D.C. 181
Blacking, John 181
 biographical details
  appearance *159*
  death 162
  education
   King's College Cambridge 161–2
   Sherborne School, Dorset 161
  friendships/collaborations
   Hugh Tracey 161
   John Baily 162
  personality 162–3
  president, Society for
   Ethnomusicology 163
  professional appointments
   Coldstream Guards 162
   International Library of African
    Music 161
   Queen's University Belfast 161
   University of Witwatersrand 161
  renown xi
 critiqued 168
  John Baily 162
  Kofi Agawu 164–9
  Reg Byron 162
 opponent of apartheid 161
 publications
  Common Sense View of All Music 161
  How Musical Is Man? 161, 167
  The Anthropology of the Body 161
  Venda Children's Songs 161, 163, 166
 research/ideas
  ethnomusicology
   anthropology 163
   fieldwork 161–3, 166
    Venda, Northern Transvaal
     161–3, 165–7
   influences 162, 166–7
   origins 161
   perspective 161, 167–9
   role in creating academic discipline
    161
  founder of European Seminar in
   Ethnomusicology 163
  human movement 162–3
  instrument morphology 162
  music structure 162
Blakey, Robert 21
Blaney, Roger 39
Bloch, Marc 134
Boas, Franz 161
Boethius, Anicius Manlius Severinus 71,
 79
Bohr, Niels 98–100
Booth, William Bramwell 51
Born, Max 98–100
Bourne, Ada 51
Braudel, Fernand 134
Brehon Law 33, 37
 Brehon Laws Commission
  (Commissioners for Publishing the
  Ancient Laws of Ireland, 1852) 33,
  40
British Academy 87, 189
British Association for the Advancement
 of Science 15, 25, 65, 125
British Library 75
British Medical Association 47
Brooke, Christopher 87
Browne, James 145
Buccleuch, Duke of 9
Buchanan, Ronald H. 138
Butler Act (1944) 177
Byron, Reg 162

Cambridge University vii, 10–11, 15,
 62, 120, 127, 161–2, 175
Cantos 110
Carmina Burana 75–6
Catholic Church opposition to Queen's
 Colleges vii–viii, 39
Census Commissioners 41
Centre for Supercomputing 189
Chanson de Roland 77
Cheney, Christopher 87
Chilver Report 121
Christianity or Europe 74
Clare College Cambridge 120, 127
Clarendon, Earl of 23
Clarke, Aidan 154
Clarke, Maud 73, 85, 89, 91–2
Clarkson, Leslie 176
Clinton, President Bill 145
College of New Jersey (later Princeton
 University); *see* Princeton University
Colportage Society of Ireland 24
Concilia 87
Connel, Kenneth 181
Connellan, Owen 37, 39
Cooke, Reverend Henry 12
Cosgrove, Art 85, 90
Council for Encouragement of Music
 and the Arts 125

INDEX

Cousin, Victor 21, 28
Cowley, Abraham 21
Crolly, William 35
Cronne, Harold 85, 90
Crossland, Sir Bernard 59, 181

Dalgarno, Alexander 146–7
Darwin, Charles 14, 16, 25–6, 61, 65
Darwinism 9, 14, 25, 28, 60–1
Davie, Donald 107–8, 110
Davis, H.W.C. 85–6, 89
Davis, Thomas 38
de Broglie, Louis 98–9
Degrees of Excellence 175–6
Deutsch, David 102
Dickie, George 25, 28
Dies Irae 76
Dixon, A.C. 72
Dolley, Michael 85
Down Survey 35
Dublin Penny Journal 33, 37
Dubourdieu, Reverend John 35
Dudley Edwards, Robin 151–2
Du Méril, Edelstand 76
Dunn, Douglas 109
Du Noyer, George 36
Durham University vii, 175

Edward II, King 91
Edward III, King 91
Einstein, Albert 98–101
Elementary Treatise on Quaternions 12
Eliot, Charles 27
Eliot, T.S. 109
Emeleus, George 95, 98, 146
Estyn Evans, Emyr xi, 181
  biographical details
    appearance *131*
    death 138
    delivers Wiles Lectures 133
    early life 133
    education
      University College Wales
        (Aberystwyth) 133–4
    family 138
    friendships/influences
      Fernand Braudel 134
      H.J. Fleure 133
      J.C. Beckett 135
      Marc Bloch 134
    health 134

  marriage 137
  professional appointments
    archaeologist 134
    Queen's University Belfast 133
  illustrator/artist 137
  publications
    Irish Heritage and Irish Folk Ways 135
    Mourne Country 135
    Prehistoric and Early Christian Ireland 134
    The Personality of Ireland 133
  research/ideas
    anthropology 133, 136
    archaeology 133, 138
    geography 133–4, 136, 138
      topography 135
    habitat 133–5, 137–8
    heritage 134–8
    history 133–5, 138
    interdisciplinary union 133–4, 137
    pastoralism 133, 135–7
    Ulster Folk and Transport Museum 137
Estyn Evans, Gwyneth 137
European Centre for Nuclear Research (CERN) 96–8
European Seminar in Ethnomusicology 163
evolution, theory of 14, 25, 28, 60–1
Ewald, Paul P. 95, 144

Famine (Great) 38–9
Fane Street Elementary School (Belfast) 95
Faraday, Michael 14, 63
Faral, Edmond 76
Feynman, Richard 102
Flanagan, Marie Therese 91
Fleure, H.J. 133
Flight of the Earls 37
folklore, scholarly interest in/promotion of 33, 35, 39, 42, 133, 135–7, 161
folk music, scholarly interest in/promotion of 39, 136; *see also* Blacking, John
Forbes, James David 10, 13
Fraser, Sir Ian 47
Friel, Brian 34
Froggatt, Sir Peter 47, 119–21, 145, 179
Fuchs, Klaus 95–6

Gaelic Revival 38
Gailey, Alan 138
Georgetown University 188
  Lannan Symposium 188
  Lombardi Cancer Centre 188
Gesta Stephani 90
Gibson, Reverend William 23
Glasscock, R.E. 154
Godwin, James 62
Goldsmith, Oliver 77
Good Friday Agreement 4, 189
Gourmont, Rémy de 76
Gown Literary Supplement 112, 125
Grant, Michael 177
Gray, Jack 85, 90–1

Haldane, R.B. 122
Hamilton, Ian 109
Hamilton, William Rowan 12
Hancock, Elizabeth 62
Hardenberg, Friedrich von (Novalis) 74
Hardiman, James 34
Harland, Edward 10
Harris, Rosemary 138
Harris, W. 36
Harvard University 27
Hays, Paul 145
Heaney, Seamus 5, 112
Heisenberg, Werner 98–100
Henry, R.M. 72
Herivel, John 144
Hewitt, John 107–9, 112
History of Galway 34
History of the County of Down 36
Hitchcock, Richard 38
Hobsbaum, Philip 112
Hopkins, William 10–11
Hume, David 26
Hunt, Richard 87
Huxley, Thomas Henry 14, 16

I mBéal Feirste Cois Cuan 39
Institute of Historical Research (University of London) 151
Inter-University Council 125–6
International Library of African Music 161
Irish Archaeological Society 33, 38
Irish Dictionary of Biography 5
Irish Historical Society 153
Irish Historical Studies 152

Irish language, scholarly interest in/promotion of 35–6, 38–42
Irish Literary Revival 108, 112
Irish Minstrelsy 34
Irish Universities Act (1908) 3, 184

Jackson, Alvin 135
Jope, Martin 181
Joule, James Prescott 13

Kane, Sir Robert 39
Keir, Sir David Lindsay 117, 174
Kelland, Philip 10
Keller, Hans 166–7
Kelvin, Lord; *see* Thomson, William
Kerr, Leslie 95
Kilkenny Archaeological Society 33
King's College Cambridge 161

Lane, Neal 145
Langton, Stephen 88
Lanyon, Charles 3
La Philosophie Écossaise 21
Larcom, Sir Thomas 34, 41
Larkin, Philip xi, 108, 161
  biographical details
    appearance *105*
    chairs Society of Authors' Eric Gregory Awards committee 113
    friendships/loves
      Kingsley Amis 108–9
      Arthur Terry 112–13
      Winifred Arnott 111
    personality 107, 109
    professional appointments
      librarian, Queen's University Belfast 107
      librarian, University of Hull 109
  broadcasts
    The Arts in Ulster (BBC) 108
  ideas/influences 107
    aestheticism 110–13
    appreciation of Hull 109, 111
    appreciation of jazz 109, 111
    appreciation of poetry 107, 109–10
      eshews academicism 107, 109–10
      eshews regionalism 109
      eshews topicality 110, 113
    hostile to Elliot–Pound hegemony 109–10
    humour 107, 109

INDEX 199

influence of Belfast 108–13
provincialism 108, 113
Romanticism 110
solitude 108–9, 111
W.B. Yeats 110, 112–13
W.H. Auden 110, 113
linked to 'the Movement' 108
poems
'Arrival' 111
'Best Society' 108
'Church-Going' 112
'Lines on a Young Lady's Photograph Album' 110–11
'The Importance of Elsewhere' 111
publications
'The Library I Came To' (*Gown Literary Supplement*) 112
Oxford Book of Twentieth Century English Verse 107
The Less Deceived 110–11
League of Nations 74
Lectures on Quaternions 12
Leerssen, Joep 37
Leinaas, Jon 97
Le Latin mystique 76
Le Pour et Contre 77
Les Fleurs du Mal 76
Locarno Pact (1925) 74
Lockwood Committee 177
Lodge, Sir Richard 89
London Academy of Music 118
London Magazine 110
Longley, Edna 161
Longley, Michael 112
Lundergårdh, Henrik 118

MacAdam, Robert Shipboy 33, 35, 39–41
MacDonald, Ramsay 74
Mackay, J.M. 88
MacNeice, Louis 112–13
Magna Carta 88
Mahon, Derek 112
Mahony, Cornelius 39
Mandl, Franz 96, 98
Mangan, James Clarence 36–7
Manon Lescaut 77
Massey, Harrie 143
Matthews, Paul 96
Maxwell, James Clerk 10, 12–13, 15
Mayer, Julius Robert 14

Mayne, Rutherford (Samuel Waddell) 77
McCosh, James vii, xi, 11
biographical details
appearance *19*
death 24
professional appointments
College of New Jersey (later Princeton Univeristy) xi, 11, 24–5, 27–8
Queen's College Belfast 21, 23, 25–8
religiosity 21–4
member of Colportage Society of Ireland 24
minister, Free Church, Brechin 22
supports Disruption of the Church of Scotland (1843) 22
publications
The Intuitions of the Mind 23
The Method of the Divine Government 22
The Scottish Philosophy 26
Typical Forms and Special Ends in Creation 25
research/ideas/influences
Baconian inductive method 21–3, 26, 28
Darwinism 25–6, 28
ethics 23, 26
evolution 24–6, 28
intuitional realism 23
metaphysics 22–3, 26
pedagogy 24–5, 27–8
plant morphology 25
psychology 25–8
Scottish Common Sense school of philosophy 21, 23, 26–8
theology 25
McCourt, Desmond 138
McCreary, Alf 175
McDonnell, James 35
McDowell, R.B. 151
McVeagh, Robert 35
Medieval Representation and Consent 92
medieval studies 85
Melville, Herman 138
Mercure de France 76
Merton College Oxford 73, 85–6
Methodist College Belfast 50–1
Meyer, Kuno 41

Migne, Jacques Paul 76
Mill, John Stuart 23
Mitchell, Senator George 189
Mitchell Symposium 189
Modus Tenendi Parliamentum 92
Mogey, John 138
Moody, T.W.
  collaborations 153–4, 174
  historiographer 151–2, 154
    'New History of Ireland' 153
  lecturer, Queen's University Belfast 90, 152, 157
  publications
    Irish Historical Studies (as contributor) 152
    Queen's Belfast, 1845–1949 3, 152–3, 173–6
    The Londonderry Plantation, 1609–41 154
  radio contributor 154
Morrison, Blake 108
Murray, John 49

National Geographic Society 188
National Institutes of Health (US) 189
National University of Ireland 3
Natural Theology 23
Nature 16
Neilson, Reverend William 35, 39
New History of Ireland 90
Newman, Cardinal John Henry 120, 175, 177
Newman's Catholic University 36, 40, 121
Newton, Isaac 14, 26, 49
Nineteenth Century Club (New York) 27
Northern Ireland Advisory Council for Education 125
Northern Ireland Assembly 187

O'Conor, Charles 33, 37
O'Curry, Eugene 36, 41
O'Daly, John 39
O'Donovan, John xi
  biographical details
    appearance 31
    awarded Cunningham Medal 38
    awarded honorary doctorate 38
    death 41
    early life 34
    education 34
    elected to Royal Prussian Academy 38
    elected to Royal Irish Academy 38
    family 41
    personality
      apparent chauvinistic attitude 39–40
      harsh critic 41
    professional appointments
      barrister 38
      Brehon Laws Commission 40
      editor/copyist 38
      Ordnance Survey 33–6, 38
      Queen's College Belfast 33, 38–40
      schoolmaster 34
      teacher of Irish 38, 40
    fieldwork (Ordnance Survey) 35–6
  publications 42
    Annála Ríoghachta Éireann (translation) 37
    Grammar of the Irish Language 38
    periodical articles
      Dublin Penny Journal 33, 37
      Ulster Journal of Archaeology 33–4
  research
    Celtic studies 36, 40, 42
    Annála Ríoghachta Éireann 37–8
    scholarly interest in Irish language 36, 40–1
    masters Old Irish 36
O'Reilly, Myles 34
Observations Upon the Prophecies of Daniel and the Apocalypse of St John 49
Ó Buachalla, Breandán 39
Ordnance Survey 33–6, 38
  topographical department 34–6, 38
Orff, Carl 75
Oriel College Oxford 86
Osborne, Henry Fairfield 24
Osler, Sir William 49
Owen, Richard 25
Owens College 175
Oxford Dictionary of National Biography 5, 129
Oxford University vii, 71, 73, 85–9, 91–2, 167, 175

Paley, William 23, 26
Palgrave, Sir Reginald 120

INDEX 201

Patrologia Latina 76
Pauli, Wolfgang 99
Peierls, Sir Rudolf 96
Petrie, George 36–8
Physical Review 100
Poésies Populaires Latines du Moyen Âge 76
Poetae Latini Carolini Aevi 76
Polytechnic Institute of Brooklyn 95
Podolsky, Boris 100
Porter, James 12
Porter, Noah 27
Porter, Reverend Josias Leslie 174
Porter, William Archer 12
Potter, G.R. 90
Pound, Ezra 109
Powicke, Sir Maurice xi, 151
  biographical details
    appearance *83*, 86
    death 86
    early life 85
  education
    Balliol College Oxford 85, 88–9
    Stockport Grammar School 85
    University of Manchester 85
  elected Fellow of British Academy 87
  elected president of Royal Historical Society 87
  friendships/collaborations
    Beryl Smalley 86
    Christopher Brooke 87
    Christopher Cheney 87
    Maud Clarke 89
    Richard Hunt 87
    Richard Southern 86
    T.F. Tout 85, 88
  knighted 86
  literary style 87–8
  personality 86–8
  professional appointments
    Balliol College Oxford 86
    Merton College Oxford 85–6
    Oriel College Oxford 86
    Queen's University 85–6, 88–9
    Regius Professor of Modern History (Oxford University) 86–7
    University of Liverpool 86, 88
    University of Manchester 86, 88–9
    War Trade Intelligence Department 89
  renown 85
  retirement 86
  publications 91
    Councils and Synods 87
    King Henry III and the Lord Edward 87
    Stephen Langton 87–8
    The Loss of Normandy 87–8
    The Thirteenth Century 87
  research/ideas
    medieval studies 85–9, 92
      intellectual development of schools 88
      Medieval Group 86, 92
      political developments 88
Presbyterian Church
  and the Irish language 39
  influence over Queen's College Belfast 51
Prévost, Abbé 77
Princeton University (formerly College of New Jersey) xi, 11, 24–5, 27–8, 146, 164
Principia 14
Principles and Practice of Medicine 49
Proudfoot, Bruce 138

Q (publication) 108
Queen's Belfast, 1845–1949 3, 152–3, 173–6
Queen's College Belfast (later Queen's University Belfast)
  academic reputation vii
  alumni 4
  curriculum 175
  elevated to university rank vii
  ethos 174
  faculties 175
  foundation vii, 176
    founding principles vii, ix, 3
  non-denominationalism 174, 176
  student body
    gender composition viii
    social-class composition viii
Queen's College Cork vii, 3, 39–40, 174
Queen's College Galway vii, 3, 39–40, 174
Queen's University Belfast (formerly Queen's College Belfast)
  academic/research reputation viii, x–xi, 3–5, 47, 85, 144–6, 163, 180–2, 185, 187–9

Institute for Electronics, Communications and Information Technology 188
Queen's University Ionic Liquids Laboratory 188
Russell Group membership 4, 187
academic collaborations
  British Academy Symposium, 'Who's Creating Knowledge?' 189
  Royal Academy of Engineering, exhibition and soirée, 'Wealth Creation through Partnership' 189
  Centre for Supercomputing 189
  Queen's–Georgetown Partnership 188
  Centre for Cancer Research and Cell Biology 188
  Trinity College Dublin 189
  University College Dublin 189
academic programme viii, ix, 47, 122, 144–5, 180
alumni 4–5
as counterweight to community division x, 117–18, 121, 176, 179, 184–5
campus 4
ethos/aims viii–xi, 122, 175, 182–3, 187–8
faculty
  'religious' composition of x, 180, 183
  gender composition of viii, x
  medical faculty, regional composition of 52
foundation vii, 3–4, 174, 176, 182
Gender Initiative viii
income/funding 178, 180–1, 184–5, 188
Institute of Lifelong Learning viii, 177
non-academic staff 183
  gender composition viii
  'religious' composition viii
publications
  Degrees of Excellence 175
'Queen's Thinkers' conference vii, 3–5, 107
relations with local community ix–x, 5, 117, 126, 179–80, 182, 185, 187
student body
  ethnic composition 122
  gender composition viii, 122, 178, 183
  numeric composition viii, 177–8, 183
  political activity 179
  regional composition 52, 122
  'religious' composition viii, 178–9, 183
  social-class composition viii, 177, 179, 183
  Student Representative Council 124, 180
Troubles, the
  attacks on college buildings 179
  murders of students/staff 179
  response/position of College 179–80, 183, 187
Queen's University of Ireland vii, 3–4, 121, 173–4
Quinn, D.B. 85, 90–1, 151–2, 157

Rediscover Northern Ireland (programme) 189
Reformation (Protestant) 37
Regnault, Victor 12
Reid, Thomas 22, 26
Reily, Suzel 163
Representing African Music 164
Research Assessment Exercise 182
Revival (religious, 1859) 13, 24
Richards, Robert 27
Richardson, H.G. 90, 92
Richardson, Samuel 77
Roberts, Michael 181
Robertson Smith, William 15
Robin, Guy 77–8
Robins Committee 176–7
  Robbins Report (1963) 176, 183
Robinson, Lennox 77
Rosen, Nathan 100
Royal Belfast Academical Institution 12–13, 39, 54, 61
Royal College of Science and Technology (later Imperial College of Science and Technology) 118
Royal Dublin Society 35
Royal Historical Society 87
Royal Institution (London) 14
Royal Irish Academy 33, 37–8, 147, 152
Royal Prussian Academy 38
Royal Society 21, 65, 103, 123, 147

Royal Society of Antiquaries of Ireland 33
Royal University of Ireland 3, 72, 174
Russell, George William (Æ) 137

Said, Edward 164
Saintsbury, George 73, 77–9
Salisbury, John of 78
Sartre, Jean-Paul 137
Sayles, Geoffrey 90–2
Schmeller, Johan Andreas 76
Schrödinger, Erwin 98–9
Scott, John 10
Scottish Enlightenment 9, 21
Scottish School of Common Sense 21, 23, 26
scribal tradition 33–4, 37
Shanks, Robin 50
Shuldham Henry, Reverend Pooley 174
Sloane, Robert Harvey 95, 98, 146
Smalley, Beryl 86
Smith, A.L. 85
Smith, Adam 9
Smith, Crosbie 59–60
Smith, Gregory 72–3, 77, 79
Smith O'Brien, William 33, 38
Social and Ethical Interpretations in Mental Development 27
Society for Ethnomusicology 163
Somerville College Oxford 73, 89
Southern, Richard 86, 88
Spear, Ruskin 119
Spitzer, Lyman 146
Spivak, Gayatri 164
St Andrew's Agreement 4
Stanford Linear Accelerator Center 97
Steele, William John 10–11
Steinberger, Jack 98
Stevelly, John 13
Stewart, Balfour 15
Stokes, Martin 162, 167–8
St Peter's College Cambridge (Peterhouse) 10–12
Swanton, Thomas 40
Synod of Thurles (opposition to Queen's Colleges) vii
System of Logic 23

Tait (née Porter), Margaret 12
Tait, Frederick 16
Tait, Peter Guthrie vii, x
  biographical details
    appearance 7, 9
    death 16
    early life 9
    education 9–10
      Circus Place School 9
      Dalkeith Grammar School 9
      Edinburgh Academy 9–10
      St Peter's College (Peterhouse) Cambridge University 10–11
      University of Edinburgh 10
    friendships/collaborations
      James Clerk Maxwell 10, 13, 15
      James Porter 12
      James Thomson (Jnr) 11–13
      John Stevelly 13
      Thomas Andrews 11, 13
      William Archer Porter 12
      William Thomson 12–15
    loss of son 16
    marriage 12
    personality 9–10, 13–14, 16
    professional appointments
      Queen's College Belfast 11, 16
      University of Edinburgh 13, 15–16
    religiosity 9, 15–16
  lectures 11, 13, 15
  publications
    A Treatise on Dynamics of a Particle 11
    Lectures on Some Recent Advances in Physical Science 15
    Thermodynamics 14
    Treatise on Natural Philosophy ('T&T') 13–14, 16
    Unseen Universe, or Physical Speculation on a Future State 15
  relations with periodical press 9, 14
  research/ideas
    chemistry of gases 11
    dynamics 16
    energy physics 13–15
    quaternions 12
    thermodynamics 14–15
    thermoelectricity 15
Taylor, A.J.P. 125
Terry, Arthur 112–13
The Arts in Ulster 108
The Chairman's Handbook 120
The Consolation of Philosophy 79
The Dark Ages 79

The Idea of a University 175
The Irish Parliament in the Middle Ages 90–1
The Movement 108
The Transition Period 73
Thompson, G.B. 138
Thomson (Jnr), James vii, xi, 11–13
  biographical details
    addresses Belfast Natural History and Philosophical Society 62
    addresses Belfast Social Inquiry Society 62
    addresses British Association for the Advancement of Science 65
    appearance 57
    death 62, 66
    delivers Royal Society's Bakerian Lecture 65
    early life 60–1
    education
      Glasgow University 61
    family 62
    health 62
    marriage 62
    professional appointments
      Belfast Water Commissioners 62, 64
      civil engineer 62
      engineer 59
      Glasgow University 59, 62
      Queen's College Belfast 12, 59, 62
      William Fairburn (shipbuilder) 62
    religiosity 59–61
    friendships/collaborations
      Michael Faraday 63
      Peter Guthrie Tait 11–13
      Thomas Andrews 63
      William Thomson 59–61, 63
  improver of urban health/environment 59–60, 62, 66
  inventor 59–60, 62–3
    centrifugal pump 63
    jet pump 63
    vortex turbine 62–3
  publications
    paper, Giant's Causeway 66
  research/ideas 13
    astronomy 66
    earth's rotation 64
    energy physics 60–1, 63–4, 66
    fluid motion 62–5
    gases to liquids 63
    geology (Giant's Causeway) 66
    glacial motion/erosion 60, 64–5
    regelation 63
    river flow 60, 64–5
    steam power 61–4
    thermodynamics 59–60, 62–3, 65
      'heat death' of the universe 60
    tides 64
    weir 62
    wind systems 60, 64–6
Thomson (Snr), James 10, 12, 15, 61
Thomson, William (Lord Kelvin) x–xi, 11–13, 15–16
  biographical details
    early life 61
    education
      Cambridge University 62
      Glasgow University 61
    eminence 59
    friendships/collaborations
      James Thomson (Jnr) 59–61, 63
      Peter Guthrie Tait 12–15
    personality 13–14
    religiosity 60–1
  publications
    Treatise on Natural Philosophy 13–14
  research/ideas 13
    electric telegraph 59
    energy physics 60–1
    geology 60–1
    ocean electric telegraphy 14
    steam power 59, 61, 63
    thermodynamics 59–63
      'heat death' of the universe 60
Todd, James Eadie 89–91, 151
Tout, T.F. 85–6, 88–9
Transactions of the Royal Irish Academy 37
Translations 34
Trinity College Dublin vii, 38, 51, 89, 103, 174, 189
Troubles, the 47, 89, 113, 157, 177–9, 187
Tyndall, John 14–15
  'Belfast Address' 15

Ulster Archaeological Society 33
Ulster Folk and Transport Museum 137
Ulster Gaelic Society 35, 39–40
Ulster Journal of Archaeology 33–4

INDEX

Ulster Literary Theatre 77
Ulster Medical Society 49, 51, 54
  Medical Institute 50–1, 54
Ulster Society for Irish Historical Studies 153
Ulsterville Avenue Elementary School (Belfast) 95
United States National Academy of Sciences 147
Université Paris-Sud Orsay 101
University College Cork vii
University College Dublin 90, 151–2
University College Galway vii
University College London 143–4
University College of Wales (Aberystwyth) 133–4
University Grants Committee (UGC) 54, 123–5, 178, 181, 184
University of Birmingham 90, 96–8, 175
University of Bristol 88, 118
University of Dublin; see Trinity College Dublin
University of Edinburgh vii, 9–10, 13, 15–16, 26, 48, 73, 89
University of Glasgow vii, 10, 12, 15, 26, 59, 61–2, 96
University of Liverpool 86, 88
University of London vii, 90, 118, 151, 175
University of Manchester 85–6, 88–9, 117, 119, 175
University of St Andrew's vii
University of Sydney 117–18
University of Texas 145
University of Ulster 121, 177, 182, 184
University of Witwatersrand 161
US–Ireland R&D Partnership Agreement 189

Vance, Norman 92
Veltman, Martinus 98
Verses Written on Several Occasions 21
Vick, Sir Arthur 124
Victoria College, Belfast 71–2
Vinogradoff, Paul 90
von Hornbostel, Erich 165
von Neumann, J. 98

Waddell, Helen xi, 92
  biographical details
    appearance 69

    delivers W.P. Ker Lecture 79
    early life 71–2
      death of parents 71
    education
      Queen's College (University) Belfast 71–3
      Royal University of Ireland 72
      Somerville College Oxford 71, 73
      Victoria College 71–2
    experience during Second World War 77–9
    friendships/collaborations
      George Saintsbury 73, 77, 79
      Gregory Smith 72, 77, 79
      Guy Robin 77–8
      Lennox Robinson 77
      Samuel Waddell (Rutherford Mayne) 77
    religiosity 72, 78–9
  lectures 73
  publications/plays
    A French Soldier Speaks 77
    Lyrics from the Chinese 71
    Manon Lescaut 77
    Medieval Latin Lyrics 74
    Peter Abelard 74
    Poetry in the Dark Ages 79
    The Abbé Prévost 77
    The Wandering Scholars 74, 76
  research/ideas
    drama 73
    European literature/lyric 71, 73–9
    Latin language/lyric/culture 71, 73–6, 78–9
    medieval literature/lyric 74, 78
    translator 71–2, 74–9
Waddell, Samuel (Rutherford Mayne) 77
Wakeman, William 36
Walker, Brian 175
Walkinshaw, Bill 96–7
Warren, Lewis 85, 91–2, 181
War Trade Intelligence Department 89
Waste Land 110
Weinstock, Lev 163
Whitla, Sir William xi
  biographical details
    appearance 45
    benefactor 50–1, 54
    death 50
    early life 48
    education

death 50
early life 48
education
    Queens University in Ireland 49
    University of Edinburgh 48
elected chairman of locaL YMca 51
elected governor of Methodist College Belfast 51
elected member of Irish Convention (1917–18) 52
elected president of Belfast Shakespeare Society 50
elected president of British Medical Association 47
elected president of Ulster Medical Society 49
elected to Westminster pliament 52
family 50
friendships
    William Bramwell Booth 51
illness 50
knighted 49
marriage 51
personality 48, 50–2, 55
politics 52
professional appointments
  Belfast General Hospital 49
  pharmaceutical chemist 48
  medical practitioner 49
  Queen's College Belfast 47, 49
religiosity 49–50, 55
renown 48–50
retirement 49
publications
  A Dictionary of Treatment or Therapeutic Index including Medical and Surgical Therapeutics 49–50
  A Manual of the Practice and Theory of Medicine 49
  Elements of Pharmacy, Materia Medica and Therapeutics 49–50
  Introductory Study on the Nature and Cause of Unbelief of Miracles and Prophecy 49–50
regionalism 53–4
research/ideas
  pedagogy 48, 51
    non-denominationalism 51
  philosophy of prescribing 50
  professional development 48–50
Wigner, Eugene 99
Williams, Alwyn 181
Windele, John 38–41
Windsor, William 91
Wise, M. Norton 60
Witherspoon, Agnes 145
Witherspoon, John 24
Wright, Thomas 76

Yale College (later University) 27
Yeats, W.B. 71, 108, 110, 112–13